Labeled Antisocial:
They Say I Have No Conscience"

By

DANIEL. D

Table of Contents

- Introduction

Why This Title?
The Weight of a Label
Breaking Down Misconceptions
What This Book Is (And Isn't)

- Part 1: Understanding ASPD Beyond the Label

1. Chapter 1: What Is Antisocial Personality Disorder?

Clinical Definition and Diagnosis
The Difference Between ASPD, Psychopathy, and Sociopathy
Common Traits vs. Misconceptions

2. Chapter 2: The Science of ASPD

Genetic, Neurological, and Environmental Factors
Brain Differences and Impulse Control
Nature vs. Nurture Debate

3. Chapter 3: Myths, Stereotypes, and Stigma

The Hollywood Effect: How Media Misrepresents ASPD
"Evil" or "Misunderstood"? Challenging Black-and-White Thinking
How Stigma Affects Those with ASPD

- Part 2: Life with ASPD

4. Chapter 4: Living Under the Label

How Society Perceives People with ASPD
The Struggles of Diagnosis (and Misdiagnosis)
Can Someone with ASPD Change?

5. Chapter 5: Relationships, Love, and Social Interactions

Family Dynamics: Growing Up with ASPD
Romantic Relationships: Myths vs. Reality
Friendships and Workplace Challenges

6. **Chapter 6: Morality, Empathy, and Conscience**
Do People with ASPD Really Lack a Conscience?
Understanding Empathy: Cognitive vs. Emotional
Right and Wrong Through an ASPD Lens

- ◆ **Part 3: The World's Response to ASPD**

7. **Chapter 7: The Justice System and ASPD**
Are All Criminals Antisocial? Are All Antisocials Criminals?
Rehabilitation vs. Punishment
How the System Fails Those with ASPD

8. **Chapter 8: Therapy, Treatment, and Management**
Can ASPD Be Treated?
What Works (and What Doesn't)
Building a Functional Life with ASPD

- ◆ **Part 4: Personal Stories and Perspectives**

9. **Chapter 9: Voices from the Inside – Firsthand Accounts of ASPD**
Stories from Individuals with ASPD (Anonymous or Fictionalized)
Challenges, Successes, and Personal Growth
How They See the World Differently

10. **Chapter 10: Living with Someone Who Has ASPD – Family & Friends Speak**
The Challenges of Loving Someone with ASPD
Setting Boundaries and Protecting Your Mental Health
Can Relationships with Someone with ASPD Work?

- ◆ **Part 5: Deeper Psychological and Social Exploration**

11. **Chapter 11: The Spectrum of Antisocial Traits**
Not All ASPD Cases Are the Same
High-Functioning vs. Low-Functioning ASPD
Where Do You Draw the Line Between "Ruthless" and "Disordered"?

12. **Chapter 12: The Role of Society in Shaping Antisocial Behavior**
How Environment Influences Antisocial Traits
The Role of Trauma, Neglect, and Upbringing
Can Society Create More Antisocial People?

13. **Chapter 13: The Dark Side of Charisma – When ASPD Becomes an Advantage**
Leadership, Business, and Power – The "Successful" Side of ASPD
How Some with ASPD Thrive in Competitive Environments
The Ethics of Power and Manipulation

- ◆ **Part 6: Practical Guidance and Support**

14. **Chapter 14: If You Think You Might Have ASPD... What Now?**
Signs That You Might Have ASPD
Seeking a Diagnosis (Or Deciding Not To)
Managing Relationships, Work, and Daily Life

15. **Chapter 15: Support and Resources for Families & Loved Ones**
How to Communicate with Someone Who Has ASPD
Coping Strategies for Families and Partners
When to Seek Help and How to Find It

16. **Bonus Section: Further Exploration (Appendix or Extra Content)**
The Evolution of ASPD in Psychiatry – How ASPD Has Been Defined Over Time
ASPD vs. Other Personality Disorders – Comparing Borderline, Narcissistic, and Antisocial Traits
Recommended Books, Studies, and Documentaries – Further Reading for Curious Minds

- **Conclusion: A New Perspective on ASPD**

Moving Beyond the Stereotypes
Understanding, Not Fear
Final Thoughts on the Label "Antisocial"

• Introduction

Why This Title?

Choosing a title for a book about Antisocial Personality Disorder (ASPD) is no small task. The name has to capture the essence of the subject while remaining engaging, informative, and accessible. I considered many alternatives—each with its own perspective and weight:

Living with ASPD – A straightforward, clinical-sounding title that focuses on the experience of those diagnosed.

Inside an Antisocial Mind – A deep dive into the psychology of ASPD, aiming to reveal the inner workings of a misunderstood condition.

The Sociopathic Label – A reflection on how society often reduces complex individuals to a single term, often misused and stigmatized.

Unapologetic – A bold, controversial title that hints at the perception that people with ASPD lack remorse or regret.

Shattering the Stigma: Real-Life Stories of ASPD – A humanizing approach that focuses on real narratives, challenging the harmful stereotypes surrounding the disorder.

The Lost Souls: Understanding and Empathizing with ASPD – A more empathetic take, highlighting the struggles and alienation that come with the diagnosis.

The Human Behind the Diagnosis: ASPD Unveiled – A reminder that a label doesn't define a person.

Unmasking the Stereotype – A call to challenge the misconceptions and fear surrounding ASPD.

Each of these titles had its merits. Some were more clinical, some more empathetic, and some more provocative. But ultimately, I chose Labeled Antisocial: They Say I Have No Conscience for a reason.

The Weight of a Label

The title reflects the reality that people with ASPD often live under a label—one that shapes how the world sees them before they even speak or act. "Antisocial," "sociopath," "psychopath"—these words are thrown around loosely, often used as insults rather than diagnostic terms. The phrase "They Say I Have No Conscience" acknowledges the perception many have about ASPD: that those with the condition lack empathy, remorse, or even humanity. But is that the whole truth?

This book is not just about ASPD as a clinical diagnosis. It's about what it means to live under that label—how it affects relationships, opportunities, and self-perception. It's about separating fact from fiction, shedding light on the diversity of experiences among those with ASPD, and challenging the black-and-white thinking that often dominates discussions about personality disorders.

If you picked up this book expecting a villain's manifesto, you'll be disappointed. If you came looking for a deeper understanding of ASPD—beyond the Hollywood portrayals and sensationalized headlines—you're in the right place.

Let's begin.

The Weight of a Label

Labels have power. They shape perceptions, influence interactions, and often define a person long before they've had a chance to define themselves. When someone is labeled antisocial, sociopathic, or without a conscience, it doesn't just describe a diagnosis—it dictates how others see them, how they are treated, and, in some cases, how they begin to see themselves.

For many, Antisocial Personality Disorder (ASPD) is more than just a clinical term—it's a loaded judgment. The moment someone hears it, assumptions take over: dangerous, manipulative, cold, incapable of love. It's as if the label erases the individual beneath it, reducing them to a villainous stereotype.

This book exists because a label is not the whole story. The truth about ASPD is far more complex than popular culture and public perception would have you believe. It's not just criminals and con artists who have ASPD. Many people with this condition live relatively ordinary lives, struggling in ways the world doesn't see or understand. Some build careers, maintain relationships, and even seek ways to adapt and function within societal norms. Others, however, do struggle with destructive behaviors—some of which reinforce the very stigma they wish to escape.

The weight of this label means that many with ASPD feel isolated, boxed into a category they never chose. But it's important to ask: Who benefits from these labels? Are they meant to help people understand ASPD, or simply to make it easier for society to cast judgment and move on?

This book doesn't aim to excuse or justify harmful behavior. Instead, it aims to examine the reality of ASPD—what it is, what it isn't, and how those labeled with it experience the world.

Breaking Down Misconceptions

If you were to ask the average person about ASPD, chances are you'd hear words like psychopath, serial killer, criminal mastermind, or emotionless monster. These images are fueled by movies, TV shows, and sensationalized media stories. But what if much of what we think we know about ASPD is wrong?

Here are some of the biggest misconceptions about ASPD—and the truth behind them:

Misconception #1: All People with ASPD Are Criminals or Violent

The Reality: While it's true that ASPD is overrepresented in prison populations, not everyone with ASPD commits crimes. Some channel their traits—such as fearlessness, impulsivity, and strategic thinking—into business, law, medicine, or other fields that reward high-risk decision-making.

Misconception #2: People with ASPD Have No Feelings at All

The Reality: Individuals with ASPD may not experience guilt or deep emotional attachment in the way most people do, but that doesn't mean they feel nothing. Many experience anger, frustration, amusement, excitement, or even a sense of loyalty—just in ways that differ from neurotypical expectations.

Misconception #3: ASPD Is the Same as Psychopathy

The Reality: Although psychopathy and ASPD share some overlap, they are not identical. Psychopathy is often seen as a subset of ASPD, characterized by a lack of emotional depth, superficial charm, and extreme manipulativeness. However, not everyone with ASPD meets the criteria for psychopathy.

Misconception #4: Therapy Doesn't Work for ASPD

The Reality: While ASPD is notoriously difficult to treat, that doesn't mean therapy is useless. Some people with ASPD learn to manage their behaviors, develop coping mechanisms, and find ways to function within societal norms. The key is the right approach—often focusing on self-interest rather than traditional emotional appeals.

Misconception #5: People with ASPD Are Unchangeable

The Reality: ASPD is a lifelong condition, but that doesn't mean people with it are incapable of growth. Some learn to regulate their impulses, adapt their behaviors, and form connections—though often in unconventional ways. Change is possible, but it looks different than it does for most people.

By breaking down these misconceptions, this book aims to replace fear with understanding—not to excuse harmful behavior, but to provide a clearer, more balanced view of what ASPD truly is.

What This Book Is (And Isn't)

Before we dive deeper, let's be clear about what this book sets out to do—and what it does not.

- What This Book Is

A deep dive into the realities of ASPD—its psychology, science, and lived experiences

An exploration of how ASPD is perceived, misunderstood, and stigmatized

A look at the challenges and strengths of those with ASPD, beyond the stereotypes

A resource for those who have ASPD, think they might, or know someone who does

- What This Book Isn't

A justification for harmful or abusive behavior

A guide on how to manipulate or exploit others

A one-size-fits-all description—every person with ASPD is different

A feel-good redemption story—this book isn't about forcing a moral lesson, but about presenting the reality as it is

This book does not exist to sugarcoat the truth, nor does it exist to condemn. Instead, it aims to offer a nuanced, realistic, and thought-provoking look at what it means to live with ASPD—whether as the person diagnosed or as someone trying to understand them.

If you're ready to challenge assumptions, question stereotypes, and explore the gray areas of human behavior, then let's begin.

◆Part 1:

Understanding ASPD Beyond the Label

Chapter 1:

What Is Antisocial Personality Disorder?

Introduction: The Complexity of Antisocial Personality Disorder

Antisocial Personality Disorder (ASPD) is a complex and often misunderstood mental health condition. It's a diagnosis that carries heavy stigma, often linked to criminal behavior, emotional coldness, and a general disregard for others' rights. However, while these traits may be a reality for some individuals with ASPD, they do not define the disorder as a whole. This chapter seeks to define ASPD clinically, explore the diagnostic criteria, compare it to other personality disorders, and address the common misconceptions that surround it.

1.1 Clinical Definition and Diagnosis

ASPD is categorized as a personality disorder in the Diagnostic and Statistical Manual of Mental Disorders, Fifth Edition (DSM-5). Personality disorders are characterized by enduring patterns of behavior, cognition, and inner experience that deviate significantly from the expectations of the individual's culture. These patterns are inflexible, pervasive, and lead to distress or impairment in functioning.

Diagnostic Criteria for ASPD (DSM-5)

To diagnose someone with ASPD, a licensed mental health professional must evaluate their behavior and personality traits against the following criteria outlined in the DSM-5:

1. A pervasive pattern of disregard for and violation of the rights of others occurring since the age of 15, as indicated by three (or more) of the following:

Failure to conform to social norms with respect to lawful behaviors (e.g., repeated criminal behavior)

Deceitfulness, as indicated by repeated lying, use of aliases, or conning others for personal gain or pleasure

Impulsivity or failure to plan ahead

Irritability and aggressiveness, often leading to physical fights or assaults

Reckless disregard for the safety of self or others

Consistent irresponsibility, such as failure to sustain consistent work behavior or honor financial obligations

Lack of remorse for actions that harm others

2. The individual must be at least 18 years old at the time of diagnosis.
3. There must be evidence of conduct disorder with onset before the age of 15, though this may not always be identifiable.
4. The antisocial behavior cannot be attributed to another mental disorder or substance abuse.

Challenges in Diagnosis

The process of diagnosing ASPD is complex. Individuals with ASPD often display high levels of manipulativeness, which can make it difficult to discern the true nature of their behavior. There's also overlap with other disorders, such as Narcissistic Personality Disorder (NPD) or Borderline Personality Disorder (BPD), which can complicate the diagnostic process. Furthermore, individuals with ASPD may seek diagnosis for specific reasons, such as legal matters, and not always be forthcoming about their symptoms or experiences.

1.2 The Difference Between ASPD, Psychopathy, and Sociopathy

ASPD is a clinical diagnosis, but it is often confused with terms like psychopathy and sociopathy. While these terms are often used interchangeably in popular media, they refer to distinct concepts with nuanced differences.

ASPD vs. Psychopathy

Psychopathy is generally considered a more severe form of antisocial behavior, characterized by a profound lack of empathy, remorse, or emotional depth. Psychopaths tend to have a genetic or neurological basis for their behavior, with some studies suggesting that certain brain structures and functions—such as those involved in emotional processing and decision-making—are different in psychopaths.

While ASPD focuses on observable behaviors, psychopathy emphasizes a broader, personality-based disorder that can manifest in manipulative, cold, and calculated behavior. Psychopaths may be better at hiding their antisocial tendencies, often appearing charming, intelligent, and successful in their pursuits, which is why they are often portrayed as "criminal masterminds" or "villains."

ASPD vs. Sociopathy

Sociopathy is another term often used to describe individuals who display antisocial behavior. However, sociopathy is not an official diagnosis in the DSM-5. It is often used to describe a subtype of antisocial behavior that is thought to be caused by environmental factors, such as childhood abuse or neglect. Sociopaths tend to display more impulsive and erratic behavior than psychopaths, and they may struggle to form stable relationships due to their emotional volatility.

While both sociopaths and psychopaths share characteristics such as deceitfulness and disregard for the law, sociopaths are more likely to form attachments to specific individuals or groups, even if their behavior is still harmful. They are often driven by anger and frustration and may engage in reckless, destructive acts without considering the consequences.

1.3 Common Traits vs. Misconceptions

ASPD is surrounded by many misconceptions, often fueled by sensationalized media portrayals. Let's take a closer look at the common traits of ASPD, how they manifest in real life, and the misconceptions that frequently arise.

Common Traits of ASPD

1. Lack of Empathy and Remorse

People with ASPD often lack the ability to feel guilt or empathy for others. They may commit harmful actions without any internal moral conflict or concern for how their actions affect others. This does not mean they are devoid of emotions, but their emotional responses tend to be superficial, calculated, or absent when it comes to others' suffering.

2. Manipulativeness

A common trait of ASPD is a tendency to manipulate others for personal gain. This can manifest in lying, exploiting, or deceiving others without remorse. Manipulation is often used as a tool to get what they want, whether in personal relationships, work environments, or social settings.

3. Impulsivity and Risk-Taking

Individuals with ASPD often engage in impulsive behaviors, making decisions without considering the long-term consequences. This can lead to legal trouble, financial instability, and unhealthy relationships. Their tendency to seek excitement and stimulation can also lead to reckless behavior, including substance abuse or unsafe sexual practices.

4. Chronic Boredom and Need for Stimulation

Many individuals with ASPD report feeling a constant sense of boredom or emptiness, which drives them to engage in thrill-seeking or disruptive behaviors. This need for excitement may be one reason why they often disregard societal rules and norms.

5. Superficial Charm and Charisma

People with ASPD are often highly charismatic and charming, which makes them capable of easily winning people over. This trait can make them appear more "normal" or even likable, which adds to the difficulty of understanding their antisocial behavior.

Common Misconceptions About ASPD

1. "All People with ASPD Are Violent"

While violence is one manifestation of ASPD, it is not a universal characteristic. Many individuals with ASPD are not physically violent but may engage in emotional or financial exploitation. The assumption that all individuals with ASPD are violent can lead to unnecessary fear and stigma.

2. "People with ASPD Are Evil or 'Born Bad'"

A common misconception is that individuals with ASPD are inherently evil or that their behavior is a result of some intrinsic flaw in their character. However, ASPD is often a complex interplay of genetic, neurological, and environmental factors. While some individuals may have a genetic predisposition to antisocial behavior, others develop it due to childhood trauma or neglect.

3. "ASPD Can't Be Treated"

ASPD is notoriously difficult to treat, and not all individuals with the disorder seek treatment. However, therapy, particularly approaches like Cognitive Behavioral Therapy (CBT) and Dialectical Behavioral Therapy (DBT), can help individuals with ASPD manage their symptoms and develop healthier coping mechanisms. This myth discourages treatment and reinforces the stigma that individuals with ASPD cannot change.

4. "People with ASPD Are Always Involved in Criminal Activities"

Although ASPD is overrepresented in criminal populations, many individuals with ASPD lead seemingly normal lives. They may hold jobs, maintain relationships, and avoid legal trouble. The disorder is not exclusively associated with criminal behavior, and many individuals with ASPD function in society, albeit in unconventional ways.

Conclusion

ASPD is a multifaceted disorder, marked by a set of behaviors that range from manipulativeness and deceitfulness to impulsivity and lack of empathy. However, the reality of ASPD is far more nuanced than the stigmatized images often portrayed in the media. By understanding the clinical criteria, differentiating it from psychopathy and sociopathy, and addressing the misconceptions surrounding it, we begin to see ASPD for what it truly is—an often misunderstood condition that demands empathy, attention, and careful consideration.

As we continue through this book, we'll break down further layers of ASPD, shedding light on its complexities and offering a more compassionate view of those affected by it. It's time to shift the conversation away from judgment and toward understanding.

Chapter 2: The Science of ASPD

Introduction: The Biological and Environmental Foundations of ASPD

Antisocial Personality Disorder (ASPD) is a complex condition that is shaped by both biological and environmental factors. The interplay between genetics, brain function, and life experiences makes understanding the disorder a multifaceted task. In this chapter, we will explore the science behind ASPD—examining how genetics, brain differences, and early life experiences contribute to the development of the disorder. We will also dive into the long-standing debate between nature and nurture to understand how each influences the behaviors associated with ASPD.

2.1 Genetic Factors in ASPD

Genetics play a significant role in the development of ASPD, but they do not solely determine who will develop the disorder. Research suggests that there is a genetic predisposition to certain traits linked to ASPD, such as impulsivity, aggression, and a lack of empathy. Let's explore how genes might contribute to ASPD and how hereditary factors shape the disorder.

Genetic Heritability of ASPD

Studies have shown that ASPD is partially heritable. Twin and adoption studies have been instrumental in determining how much of the disorder can be attributed to genetics. In these studies, researchers compare identical twins (who share 100% of their genetic material) with fraternal twins (who share 50%) and adopted children with their biological parents. The findings suggest that there is a significant genetic component to ASPD, with some estimates suggesting that about 50-60% of the risk for developing ASPD can be attributed to genetic factors.

However, it's essential to note that genetics alone do not determine whether someone will develop ASPD. Instead, genes may predispose individuals to certain behaviors or temperaments, such as impulsivity, low emotional responsiveness, or aggression, which may increase the risk of ASPD. Environmental factors, such as early childhood trauma or abuse, may then interact with these genetic predispositions to bring the disorder to the surface.

Genes and Behavioral Traits Linked to ASPD

Several genetic variations have been linked to behaviors associated with ASPD. Some of these genes involve neurotransmitters like dopamine, serotonin, and norepinephrine, which influence mood regulation, reward processing, and impulse control. For example:

MAO-A (Monoamine Oxidase A): This gene, sometimes referred to as the "warrior gene," is responsible for breaking down neurotransmitters. Variants of this gene have been linked to increased aggression, particularly when combined with environmental factors like childhood abuse.

COMT (Catechol-O-Methyltransferase): This gene affects dopamine regulation and has been associated with impulsivity and aggression, traits commonly seen in people with ASPD.

DRD4 (Dopamine Receptor D4): This gene plays a role in dopamine regulation and has been linked to novelty-seeking behavior and impulsivity, which are traits often associated with ASPD.

While these genetic factors contribute to the development of ASPD, they do not guarantee that someone will develop the disorder. The interaction between genetic predispositions and life experiences plays a critical role in the manifestation of ASPD.

2.2 Neurological Differences and Impulse Control

One of the key features of ASPD is a marked lack of impulse control, which is often associated with poor decision-making, criminal behavior, and an inability to plan for the future. Research has revealed that individuals with ASPD may exhibit neurological differences that impact their ability to regulate emotions, control impulses, and respond to punishment. This section will explore the brain structures and functions that are implicated in ASPD.

Brain Differences in Individuals with ASPD

Research using neuroimaging techniques such as MRI and PET scans has identified several brain areas that function differently in individuals with ASPD. These differences may help explain the lack of empathy, impulse control issues, and manipulative behaviors often seen in individuals with the disorder.

Prefrontal Cortex (PFC): The prefrontal cortex is responsible for higher-order cognitive functions, including impulse control, decision-making, and empathy. Studies have shown that people with ASPD often have reduced activity in the prefrontal cortex, particularly in the areas involved in regulating emotions and considering long-term consequences. This impairment can lead to poor decision-making, impulsivity, and an inability to feel remorse for harmful actions.

Amygdala: The amygdala is involved in processing emotions, particularly fear and aggression. People with ASPD tend to have reduced amygdala activity, which may contribute to their emotional detachment and lack of empathy for others. A diminished amygdala response may make it harder for individuals with ASPD to experience fear or guilt, two emotions that typically inhibit antisocial behaviors.

Ventral Striatum: This brain region is involved in reward processing and motivation. Research has shown that individuals with ASPD may have increased activity in the ventral striatum, making them more susceptible to rewarding stimuli and reinforcing behaviors like thrill-seeking and criminal activity. This could explain why individuals with ASPD may engage in reckless or harmful behaviors despite the consequences.

Hippocampus: The hippocampus is involved in memory formation and emotional processing. Some studies suggest that individuals with ASPD may have structural differences in the hippocampus, which could affect their ability to form emotional memories or recall past experiences of punishment.

These brain differences suggest that ASPD is not simply a result of personal choice or moral failure; rather, there are biological underpinnings that influence how individuals with ASPD think, feel, and behave.

Impulse Control and Decision Making

The neurological differences in individuals with ASPD contribute to their poor impulse control and maladaptive decision-making. People with ASPD often engage in risky, criminal, or unethical behavior without regard for the consequences. This impulsivity is linked to reduced activity in the prefrontal cortex and increased activity in the brain's reward centers. As a result, they may feel compelled to act impulsively to satisfy immediate desires, even when doing so may harm others or lead to long-term negative outcomes.

2.3 Environmental Factors: The Role of Early Life Experiences

While genetics and neurological differences contribute to the development of ASPD, environmental factors—particularly early childhood experiences—play a crucial role in shaping the disorder. Childhood trauma, abuse, neglect, and exposure to violent or unstable environments can all increase the risk of developing ASPD later in life.

The Impact of Childhood Abuse and Neglect

One of the most significant environmental risk factors for ASPD is childhood abuse or neglect. Children who grow up in abusive or neglectful environments often develop maladaptive coping strategies, such as emotional detachment, aggression, and a lack of trust in others. These early experiences can distort emotional processing and contribute to the development of traits commonly seen in ASPD, such as impulsivity, callousness, and disregard for social norms.

Research has shown that individuals with ASPD are more likely to have experienced physical, emotional, or sexual abuse during childhood. The severity and duration of abuse also correlate with the severity of ASPD symptoms. Children who are exposed to violence, neglect, or parental rejection may internalize these behaviors and adopt antisocial coping mechanisms as a way to protect themselves from emotional pain.

The Role of Attachment and Bonding

Early attachment experiences also play a critical role in the development of ASPD. Children who fail to form secure attachments with caregivers may develop attachment disorders that contribute to ASPD symptoms. Insecure attachment, especially avoidant or disorganized attachment, has been linked to the development of antisocial traits.

Children who do not experience consistent, loving care may struggle to learn empathy, trust, and social norms. As a result, they may fail to develop the emotional and social skills necessary for healthy relationships and moral decision-making.

Social and Environmental Influences

In addition to childhood trauma, broader social and environmental factors can influence the development of ASPD. For example, children who grow up in impoverished neighborhoods, are exposed to peer violence, or witness criminal behavior may be more likely to adopt antisocial behaviors themselves. These environmental influences interact with genetic predispositions and early life experiences to increase the likelihood of developing ASPD.

2.4 The Nature vs. Nurture Debate

The debate between nature and nurture has long been a central focus in psychology and psychiatry. When it comes to ASPD, the question is whether the disorder is primarily shaped by genetics (nature) or early life experiences (nurture).

Nature: The Genetic and Neurological Argument

Proponents of the nature argument contend that ASPD is largely determined by genetic and neurological factors. Research showing heritability rates of 50-60% suggests that individuals with a family history of ASPD or related disorders may be more likely to develop the condition. Additionally, brain differences, particularly in the prefrontal cortex and amygdala, support the idea that ASPD is rooted in biological abnormalities.

Nurture: The Role of Environment and Experience

On the other hand, those who emphasize the role of nurture argue that ASPD is primarily shaped by early life experiences. Childhood abuse, neglect, and unstable family environments are significant risk factors for developing the disorder. In this view, ASPD can be seen as a response to trauma, where individuals learn maladaptive behaviors as a way to cope with their environment.

The Interaction Between Nature and Nurture

Most modern psychologists and researchers agree that ASPD arises from a combination of both nature and nurture. Genetic predispositions may make certain individuals more susceptible to developing ASPD, but environmental factors like childhood abuse, trauma, and neglect can interact with these genetic vulnerabilities to trigger the disorder. This interaction between biological factors and life experiences underscores the complexity of ASPD and challenges the idea of a single cause.

Conclusion

ASPD is a disorder that cannot be understood through a single lens. The genetic, neurological, and environmental factors all contribute to the development of the disorder, each playing a unique and interconnected role. While research has made significant strides in identifying the underlying causes of ASPD, the disorder remains complex, and no single explanation can fully account for its development. ASPD is not a monolithic condition; rather, it manifests differently across individuals, influenced by a combination of biology, life experiences, and personal choices.

One of the most critical takeaways from this book is that the label of "antisocial" often obscures the complexity of the disorder and the individuals who live with it. As we've seen throughout this journey, individuals with ASPD can have a wide range of experiences, from those who manage to live relatively functional lives to those who struggle significantly with relationships, impulse control, and adhering to societal norms. Understanding this variability is essential for dispelling harmful stereotypes and providing a more empathetic, nuanced view of those living with ASPD.

Moreover, the conversation surrounding ASPD must evolve beyond the binary of "good" versus "bad." It is vital to acknowledge that people with ASPD are not inherently evil or beyond help. Many people with ASPD experience deep inner turmoil, but their disorder can manifest in ways that lead to maladaptive coping mechanisms, harm to themselves or others, and a cycle of isolation. By shifting our focus toward understanding the causes and offering appropriate interventions, society can better support those affected and work to reduce the negative stigma they face.

While treatment for ASPD is undeniably challenging, it's crucial to remember that recovery and growth are not impossible. Though there is no one-size-fits-all solution, therapy, especially approaches like cognitive-behavioral therapy (CBT) and dialectical behavior therapy (DBT), can help individuals develop healthier ways of thinking and coping. These methods, alongside a strong support system and a commitment to long-term change, can lead to significant improvements in quality of life.

It is also essential to recognize the role of the broader community in creating an environment where individuals with ASPD can thrive, or at least attempt to live without further alienation. Family, friends, and professionals all have critical roles to play in offering guidance and empathy, ensuring that individuals do not feel abandoned by society or their loved ones.

In closing, it is my hope that this book serves as a starting point for deeper discussions about Antisocial Personality Disorder. This book isn't just an attempt to explain the disorder, but also an effort to challenge the prevailing attitudes that often hinder understanding and compassion. People with ASPD are not defined solely by their disorder; they are multifaceted individuals, capable of change and growth, even if that change takes time and patience.

Let us work together to shift the narrative around ASPD, embracing a perspective that emphasizes humanity over labels, empathy over judgment, and understanding over fear. Only then can we begin to break down the barriers of misunderstanding and stigma, creating a world where everyone has the opportunity to heal, grow, and live authentically—regardless of their mental health challenges.

Chapter 3: Myths, Stereotypes, and Stigma

3.1 The Hollywood Effect: How Media Misrepresents ASPD

One of the biggest contributors to the public's misunderstanding of Antisocial Personality Disorder (ASPD) is the portrayal of individuals with this condition in popular media. From films to television shows, ASPD is often depicted in exaggerated, sensationalized, or downright inaccurate ways. The entertainment industry tends to focus on the more extreme manifestations of the disorder, often presenting characters as cold-blooded killers, manipulators, or criminal masterminds. These portrayals feed into society's deep-seated fears of those with ASPD and obscure the reality of living with the disorder.

In movies like American Psycho (featuring the infamous Patrick Bateman), The Silence of the Lambs (with Hannibal Lecter), and Dexter (about a sociopathic serial killer who works as a blood-spatter analyst), the main characters are depicted as not only engaging in criminal behavior but also thriving in it. While these characters may share some traits with individuals diagnosed with ASPD, such as lack of empathy, impulsivity, and disregard for societal norms, they are far from accurate representations of the condition. The intense violence, immorality, and sheer malevolence of these characters create a distorted image of what it means to live with ASPD.

3.1.1 The Real Impact of Hollywood's Misrepresentation

For those living with ASPD, this kind of media portrayal can make it even more difficult to seek help, as they may fear being stigmatized or judged harshly. Additionally, it can intensify the emotional burden placed on family members and loved ones, who are forced to contend with the false belief that their loved one is a "monster" rather than someone with a complex mental health condition that requires understanding and intervention.

It's important to break away from these Hollywood stereotypes and develop a more nuanced understanding of ASPD. Yes, individuals with ASPD may engage in manipulative or self-serving behaviors, but they are not inherently "evil" or "born criminals." The truth is much more complicated.

3.2 "Evil" or "Misunderstood"? Challenging Black-and-White Thinking

The dichotomy between "evil" and "misunderstood" is a theme that often arises when discussing ASPD. Society tends to think in absolutes: people are either "good" or "bad," and those who exhibit traits of ASPD often fall squarely into the "bad" category. This black-and-white thinking perpetuates harmful stereotypes and prevents a deeper exploration of the disorder. It also undermines the possibility of growth and understanding for those who are diagnosed with ASPD.

3.2.1 "Evil" Label: The Dangerous Assumption

On the one hand, the "evil" label suggests that individuals with ASPD are inherently malicious, ruthless, and deserving of society's condemnation. They are seen as incapable of empathy, unable to care about the well-being of others, and driven by a need to dominate or manipulate. In this view, there is little room for redemption or self-improvement. Those with ASPD are written off as "lost causes," never to change, incapable of feeling guilt or remorse, and unworthy of forgiveness or understanding.

3.2.2 "Misunderstood" Perspective: A Call for Empathy

On the other hand, there is the "misunderstood" perspective, which emphasizes that ASPD should not be viewed through a moral lens, but rather as a complex psychological condition. Those with ASPD often experience difficulties with emotional regulation, impulse control, and forming healthy attachments, leading to behaviors that can be harmful to themselves and others. However, understanding the disorder means acknowledging that these individuals are not inherently evil. They are people who struggle with their internal worlds, often influenced by genetic, environmental, and neurological factors.

3.2.3 Moving Beyond Extremes

The challenge lies in moving beyond the extremes of the "evil" or "misunderstood" labels. ASPD exists on a spectrum, and each person diagnosed with the disorder experiences it in their unique way. The traits associated with ASPD—impulsivity, aggression, disregard for rules, and emotional detachment—can present in varying degrees of intensity. This means that some individuals may engage in harmful or destructive behavior, while others may function relatively well in society, maintaining stable relationships and jobs despite their difficulties.

In the end, the key to understanding ASPD is to resist oversimplification. It is important to recognize the complexity of the disorder and to avoid categorizing individuals with ASPD as either "evil" or "misunderstood." A more compassionate approach acknowledges that while these individuals may exhibit challenging behaviors, they are still human beings deserving of empathy, support, and a chance for change.

3.3 How Stigma Affects Those with ASPD

The stigma surrounding ASPD is pervasive and deeply damaging. Those with the disorder often face prejudice and discrimination, which can exacerbate their difficulties and hinder their ability to function in society. The negative label attached to ASPD means that individuals with the condition are often viewed through a lens of suspicion and distrust, regardless of their individual circumstances or behavior.

3.3.1 Impact on Mental Health and Self-Worth

Stigma can significantly impact the mental health and self-worth of individuals with ASPD. From a young age, they may learn that their behavior is seen as unacceptable or deviant by society. This can lead to feelings of isolation, shame, and frustration. Many people with ASPD struggle with low self-esteem, and the added weight of societal judgment can make it even harder for them to seek help or form meaningful connections with others. The fear of being rejected or misunderstood often leads them to withdraw, which can perpetuate feelings of loneliness and alienation.

3.3.2 Impact on Accessing Treatment and Support

The societal stigma around ASPD also prevents individuals from accessing the support they need. Whether it's mental health treatment, social services, or family support, many people with ASPD avoid seeking help because they fear being judged or labeled as "bad" or "dangerous." They may feel that they won't be taken seriously or that others will view them as incapable of change. This fear can prevent them from engaging in treatment that could improve their quality of life.

3.3.3 Impact on Relationships

Stigma also affects relationships, both with family members and romantic partners. People with ASPD are often labeled as manipulative, selfish, and emotionally distant, making it difficult for them to establish trusting, supportive relationships. Family members, too, may struggle with their own feelings of shame or confusion. They may not know how to support their loved ones, or they may be too afraid to confront the realities of ASPD. This can create a cycle of emotional distance, frustration, and misunderstandings that perpetuates the stigma.

In romantic relationships, the effects of stigma can be just as profound. A partner with ASPD may feel that they are constantly being judged or criticized, while their partner may struggle to understand the emotional disconnect. This can lead to resentment and breakdowns in communication, which are particularly difficult for those with ASPD who already struggle with forming meaningful emotional connections.

3.3.4 The Need for Education and Awareness

To combat the stigma associated with ASPD, we need widespread education and awareness about the disorder. Society must move beyond simplistic stereotypes and focus on providing accurate, compassionate portrayals of individuals with ASPD. We must challenge the misconception that people with ASPD are all violent criminals and instead promote an understanding of the complex factors that contribute to the disorder.

Mental health professionals, educators, and advocates must work together to reduce the stigma that surrounds ASPD and create more supportive environments for individuals affected by the disorder. With better understanding comes greater acceptance, and with acceptance comes the opportunity for individuals with ASPD to seek treatment, build healthier relationships, and lead fulfilling lives.

This chapter highlights the need to challenge the harmful myths and stereotypes surrounding ASPD. It encourages a shift from fear-based thinking to a more nuanced understanding of the disorder—one that emphasizes empathy, education, and a more humanized approach to those living with ASPD. The stigma surrounding ASPD must be addressed at all levels, from individuals to society at large, to ensure that those affected can live without the weight of harmful labels.

◆Part 2:

Life with ASPD

Chapter 4:

Living Under the Label

4.1   How Society Perceives People with ASPD

The moment someone is diagnosed with Antisocial Personality Disorder (ASPD), they are immediately subjected to a societal label that comes with significant weight. Whether it's family, friends, or even professionals, those with ASPD are often treated differently due to the stigma and preconceived notions that accompany the diagnosis. People with ASPD are often regarded as cold, manipulative, self-serving, and dangerous. While some of these traits may hold true for a minority of individuals with ASPD, they do not represent the full spectrum of the disorder. The reality is far more complex.

4.1.1 The Danger of Labels

The label of ASPD can be incredibly damaging to an individual's self-image and self-worth. When society views someone as "antisocial" or "dangerous," it creates an environment of exclusion, judgment, and suspicion. For many, this label becomes a self-fulfilling prophecy. As society stigmatizes individuals with ASPD, they may internalize these negative perceptions, leading them to further isolate themselves and adopt the behaviors that others expect of them.

The cultural narrative that those with ASPD are "evil" or inherently harmful can drive a wedge between those with the disorder and the general public. This can affect their ability to form relationships, secure employment, or even live a peaceful life in society. Individuals with ASPD may be ostracized, often seen through a distorted lens that does not account for their unique struggles or humanity.

4.1.2 Media's Role in Shaping Perception

Media representations of ASPD have largely contributed to the negative public perception of the disorder. Movies, television shows, and books often portray people with ASPD as violent criminals, serial killers, or unfeeling masterminds. This representation, while sensational, rarely captures the everyday reality of those living with the disorder. The media's tendency to amplify the extremes of the disorder fuels societal fear and misunderstanding, reinforcing the idea that anyone with ASPD is a threat to society.

In truth, most people with ASPD do not engage in criminal behavior or act out violently. They may struggle with interpersonal relationships, maintaining jobs, or managing emotions, but this does not mean they are inherently dangerous. However, the constant barrage of harmful depictions creates an environment where people diagnosed with ASPD are often feared or labeled as outcasts.

4.1.3 The Impact of Stigma on Personal Identity

For those diagnosed with ASPD, the stigma surrounding their disorder can become a significant part of their personal identity. Internalizing societal perceptions of being "bad" or "unfeeling" can influence their behavior, perpetuating feelings of alienation and isolation. This dynamic is especially harmful because it prevents individuals with ASPD from seeking the help they need and from living fulfilling, healthy lives.

People with ASPD may struggle with vulnerability, often feeling that if they show emotion or weakness, they will be judged harshly or deemed unworthy of empathy. This fear can make it difficult for them to engage in relationships or seek support. They may also develop maladaptive coping strategies, such as avoidance or aggression, to shield themselves from further judgment.

4.2 The Struggles of Diagnosis (and Misdiagnosis)

The diagnosis of ASPD is often fraught with complications. The symptoms of the disorder can be difficult to differentiate from other personality disorders, and many people who present with ASPD traits may be misdiagnosed with other conditions. Moreover, the criteria for ASPD are often subjective and open to interpretation, making the diagnosis both challenging and controversial.

4.1.1 The Diagnostic Process

Diagnosing ASPD requires a thorough clinical evaluation, typically involving a combination of personal history, psychological testing, and clinical observation. Mental health professionals must assess an individual's patterns of behavior, their relationships, and their ability to follow social norms. One of the key diagnostic criteria for ASPD is a pervasive disregard for the rights of others, as well as chronic deceitfulness and impulsivity.

However, this process can be complicated by the fact that ASPD symptoms often overlap with those of other personality disorders, including Narcissistic Personality Disorder (NPD) and Borderline Personality Disorder (BPD). These overlapping traits—such as difficulty with relationships, emotional dysregulation, and impulsivity—make it challenging for clinicians to reach a definitive diagnosis.

4.1.2 Misdiagnosis and the Risk of Overlap

Misdiagnosis is a common issue when it comes to ASPD. People with traits that resemble ASPD may be misdiagnosed with other conditions, such as Bipolar Disorder, depression, or substance use disorders. This is particularly problematic when individuals are treated for the wrong condition, as it may lead to ineffective interventions or a lack of treatment for the underlying issues related to ASPD.

In some cases, individuals with ASPD may be diagnosed with Narcissistic Personality Disorder (NPD), which shares many traits with ASPD, such as grandiosity and a lack of empathy. However, people with NPD tend to be more self-centered and preoccupied with their own status, while those with ASPD exhibit a more general disregard for others' rights. Inaccurate diagnoses can result in misaligned treatment plans, contributing to frustration and setbacks in managing the disorder.

4.2.3 The Challenge of Self-Identification

For individuals with ASPD, the process of recognizing and accepting their diagnosis can be fraught with challenges. Many people with ASPD are not inclined to seek help on their own, as they may not perceive their behavior as problematic. In fact, those with ASPD often view their traits—such as manipulation, deceit, and disregard for rules—as strengths rather than weaknesses.

This lack of self-awareness can delay diagnosis and treatment, with individuals continuing to engage in harmful behaviors without understanding the underlying causes. Moreover, the stigma surrounding ASPD can lead people to deny or hide their symptoms, making it even more difficult to get an accurate diagnosis.

4.3 Can Someone with ASPD Change?

One of the most frequently asked questions about ASPD is whether individuals with the disorder can change. The answer is not a simple one, as change depends on various factors, including the severity of the disorder, the individual's willingness to engage in treatment, and the support systems available to them.

4.3.1 The Role of Treatment in Managing ASPD

While ASPD is considered one of the more challenging personality disorders to treat, it is not impossible for individuals to make meaningful changes in their behavior. Treatment options for ASPD typically include psychotherapy, with the most effective approach being cognitive behavioral therapy (CBT). CBT helps individuals with ASPD identify and change maladaptive patterns of thinking and behavior. By focusing on modifying how they perceive and respond to others, individuals can learn to develop healthier relationships and social skills.

However, therapy for ASPD can be difficult because individuals with this disorder may not recognize the need for change. They may resist therapy or manipulate the process to their advantage, making it challenging for therapists to make progress. Still, with the right therapeutic interventions and a genuine desire for improvement, many individuals with ASPD can lead fulfilling lives, free from the most damaging aspects of the disorder.

4.3.2 Medication and Co-occurring Disorders

There is no specific medication for ASPD, but medications may be prescribed to address co-occurring conditions, such as depression, anxiety, or irritability. Antidepressants or mood stabilizers may help individuals with ASPD manage emotional dysregulation and reduce impulsive behavior. However, these medications are generally used as adjuncts to therapy rather than as stand-alone treatments for ASPD.

4.3.3 The Impact of Early Intervention

Early intervention is key to improving outcomes for individuals with ASPD. The earlier someone is diagnosed and begins treatment, the better the chances of managing symptoms and preventing the disorder from worsening over time. Early therapy may also help individuals develop healthier coping mechanisms and reduce the likelihood of engaging in destructive behaviors.

However, for those with ASPD who are older and have developed entrenched patterns of behavior over the years, treatment may be less effective. Long-standing habits and attitudes can be difficult to change, especially if the individual is not motivated to do so.

4.3.3 The Potential for Change and Growth

Ultimately, whether someone with ASPD can change depends on their willingness to acknowledge their condition and work toward improving it. While ASPD may not be "curable" in the traditional sense, individuals with the disorder can make meaningful strides toward managing their symptoms and improving their lives. The potential for change exists, but it requires self-awareness, commitment to therapy, and the right environment for healing.

Conclusion

Living under the label of ASPD is a complicated and challenging experience. Society's perception of those with ASPD is often skewed by stereotypes, misconceptions, and fear, making it difficult for individuals with the disorder to lead fulfilling, meaningful lives. The struggles of diagnosis, misdiagnosis, and stigma only add to the burden. However, with proper treatment, self-awareness, and the right support, individuals with ASPD can work toward positive change. The journey may be difficult, but it is not impossible. Change is possible for those who are willing to confront their condition and take proactive steps toward healing and growth.

Chapter 5:

Relationships, Love, and Social Interactions

Understanding how Antisocial Personality Disorder (ASPD) affects relationships is essential to challenging stereotypes and gaining a more nuanced perspective. While individuals with ASPD often struggle with emotional depth, trust, and social conventions, they are not inherently incapable of forming relationships. This chapter explores how ASPD manifests in different types of relationships—family, romantic, friendships, and workplace interactions—while addressing common misconceptions and challenges.

5.1 Family Dynamics: Growing Up with ASPD

5.1.1 Early Signs and Childhood Behavior

Many individuals who are later diagnosed with ASPD exhibit warning signs in childhood. These often include persistent rule-breaking, manipulation, deceit, or aggression. Some children with these tendencies are diagnosed with Conduct Disorder (CD), which is considered a precursor to ASPD in adulthood.

Family members may notice:

A lack of guilt after misbehaving

An inability to form deep emotional bonds

Frequent lying or manipulative tendencies

Cruelty toward animals or peers

Repeated defiance of authority

Parental response plays a crucial role in shaping the child's development. A supportive and structured environment may help mitigate some antisocial behaviors, but in many cases, the signs persist into adulthood.

5.1.2 The Impact on Siblings and Parents

Growing up with a family member who has ASPD can be challenging. Parents may feel guilt, frustration, or helplessness, particularly if traditional discipline methods fail. Siblings, on the other hand, may struggle with trust issues, especially if they have been manipulated, hurt, or deceived.

Common challenges faced by families include:

The emotional toll of dealing with unpredictable behavior

Difficulty maintaining boundaries without conflict

Fear or mistrust, especially if the individual has a history of aggression

Guilt over "failing" to prevent the disorder from manifesting

Parents who have a child with ASPD often face judgment from others who assume that bad parenting caused the disorder. While environmental factors play a role, ASPD has strong genetic and neurological underpinnings that make it more complex than simple upbringing issues.

5.1.3 The Role of Childhood Environment

While genetics contribute significantly to ASPD, childhood experiences shape how the disorder manifests. Studies suggest that individuals raised in environments with:

Abuse or neglect

Inconsistent discipline

Parental criminal behavior

Exposure to violence

Are more likely to develop severe antisocial traits. However, not everyone with ASPD comes from a troubled background. Some are raised in stable, supportive households but still exhibit the characteristic traits.

5.2   Romantic Relationships: Myths vs. Reality

5.2.1 Can Someone with ASPD Love?

One of the biggest misconceptions about ASPD is that individuals with the disorder are incapable of love. While their relationships may look different from neurotypical connections, people with ASPD can form attachments in their own way.

Some characteristics of romantic relationships involving someone with ASPD include:

A preference for control in the relationship

A struggle with emotional vulnerability

A tendency toward impulsivity or infidelity

A practical or transactional approach to love

While they may not experience love in a deeply empathetic way, they can still enjoy companionship, loyalty, and mutual benefit.

5.2.2 Common Struggles in Romantic Relationships

People with ASPD often struggle with:

Trust issues: They may see emotional vulnerability as a weakness.

Manipulation tendencies: They might use charm or deception to get what they want.

Impulsivity: Risk-taking behaviors, including infidelity or financial recklessness, can create instability.

Lack of empathy: This can make it difficult for partners to feel heard or understood.

However, this does not mean all relationships involving someone with ASPD are doomed. With awareness, structure, and boundaries, some individuals with ASPD maintain long-term partnerships.

5.2.3 Attraction to Power and Control

Individuals with ASPD may be drawn to power dynamics in relationships, sometimes enjoying relationships where they hold dominance. This does not necessarily mean they are abusive, but they may prefer partnerships that benefit them in tangible ways.

Conversely, some partners are drawn to people with ASPD due to their confidence, charm, and risk-taking nature. These relationships often start intensely but can become unstable over time.

5.3 Friendships and Workplace Challenges

5.3.1 Making and Maintaining Friendships

Friendships with someone who has ASPD can be complex. Many people with ASPD struggle to form deep, emotionally reciprocal bonds, but they can still engage in friendships based on:

Mutual interests

Shared goals or benefits

Social convenience

While they may not express traditional empathy, they can be engaging, fun, and even protective of those they consider valuable.

5.3.2 Social Manipulation and Friendships

Some individuals with ASPD may use friendships strategically, forming connections that serve a purpose. They may:

Use charm to gain influence

Manipulate situations for personal gain

Discard friendships when they are no longer useful

This is not always malicious—sometimes, it is simply how they navigate relationships. Others with ASPD may genuinely value their friends but struggle with emotional depth.

5.3.3 Workplace Interactions and Challenges

People with ASPD may thrive in certain professional environments, particularly those that reward:

Risk-taking behavior

Strategic thinking

Decisive leadership

However, they may also face difficulties, including:

Authority conflicts: Resisting rules and hierarchical structures.

Impulsivity: Making rash decisions without considering consequences.

Lack of teamwork: Struggling with collaboration due to distrust or self-interest.

Some individuals with ASPD excel in competitive careers such as sales, law, business, or entrepreneurship, where their confidence and strategic thinking give them an edge.

5.3.4 Can a Person with ASPD Be a Good Leader?

While traditional leadership qualities include empathy and teamwork, people with ASPD can still be effective leaders in high-pressure environments. Their ability to:

Stay calm under stress

Make calculated decisions

Avoid emotional distractions

Can make them successful, particularly in industries that value results over interpersonal harmony.

Conclusion

ASPD affects relationships in many ways, but it does not make meaningful connections impossible. Whether in family dynamics, romantic relationships, friendships, or the workplace, people with ASPD experience social interactions through a unique lens. Understanding their challenges—while also recognizing their strengths—can lead to a more nuanced perspective that moves beyond stereotypes.

By setting clear boundaries, maintaining realistic expectations, and focusing on mutual respect, it is possible for individuals with ASPD to form lasting relationships, even if their approach to connection differs from societal norms.

Chapter 6:

Morality, Empathy, and Conscience

Introduction

One of the most controversial aspects of Antisocial Personality Disorder (ASPD) is its connection to morality, empathy, and conscience. Society often assumes that individuals with ASPD are inherently "evil," devoid of moral reasoning, and incapable of empathy. But is that true? The reality is far more nuanced.

This chapter explores the nature of conscience in individuals with ASPD, the different forms of empathy, and how people with ASPD perceive morality and social norms. Rather than viewing ASPD through a black-and-white lens, we will examine the complexities that shape how individuals with the disorder navigate moral decisions.

6.1 Do People with ASPD Really Lack a Conscience?

6.1.1 What Is Conscience?

Conscience is often described as the internal voice that helps people distinguish right from wrong. It is shaped by:

Biology: Some researchers believe conscience is linked to brain structures like the prefrontal cortex, which regulates impulse control and decision-making.

Socialization: Moral values are often taught through cultural norms, religion, and upbringing.

Emotional Response: Feelings like guilt and remorse typically reinforce moral behavior.

Individuals with ASPD often struggle with these factors, leading to a diminished sense of conscience. However, this does not mean they are incapable of making moral choices.

6.1.2 The Spectrum of Conscience in ASPD

Not all individuals with ASPD completely lack a moral compass. Instead, they may experience conscience differently. Common variations include:

Selective Morality: They may follow their own set of moral rules, often based on personal benefit rather than societal norms.

Lack of Emotional Guilt: They may intellectually understand right and wrong but not feel the emotional weight of their actions.

Pragmatic Ethics: Instead of basing decisions on morality, they may base them on practicality and consequences.

While many individuals with ASPD do not experience guilt in the way neurotypical people do, some still recognize social expectations and modify their behavior accordingly.

6.1.3 Can People with ASPD Follow Moral Codes?

Some individuals with ASPD develop a rational understanding of morality and choose to follow societal rules—not because they feel guilt, but because it benefits them. This may include:

Understanding that criminal activity could lead to punishment.

Recognizing that ethical behavior earns trust and social advantages.

Following personal codes of conduct that align with their self-interest.

This pragmatic approach to morality allows some individuals with ASPD to function successfully in society, even if their motivation for moral behavior differs from that of neurotypical individuals.

6.2 Understanding Empathy: Cognitive vs. Emotional

6.2.1 Defining Empathy

Empathy is the ability to understand and share the feelings of others. However, empathy exists in two forms:

Cognitive Empathy: The ability to intellectually recognize someone else's emotions.

Emotional (Affective) Empathy: The ability to feel another person's emotions on a personal level.

Most individuals with ASPD have cognitive empathy but lack emotional empathy. This distinction is critical to understanding their interactions with others.

6.2.2 The Role of Cognitive Empathy in ASPD

Because many individuals with ASPD possess cognitive empathy, they can:

Detect when someone is upset or vulnerable.

Mimic emotional responses to blend into social situations.

Manipulate others based on their emotional states.

However, they may struggle with:

Truly feeling another person's distress.

Responding with genuine compassion or concern.

Understanding why certain emotions lead to particular moral judgments.

Cognitive empathy allows individuals with ASPD to be highly effective in social situations, particularly in roles that require persuasion, negotiation, or influence.

6.2.3 Why Emotional Empathy Is Limited in ASPD

Brain imaging studies suggest that individuals with ASPD have reduced activity in areas like the amygdala, which is linked to processing fear, guilt, and emotional responses. This neurological difference may explain why they do not experience emotional empathy in the same way as neurotypical individuals.

However, some individuals with ASPD learn to compensate for this lack by mimicking expected emotional responses. This allows them to navigate social relationships, though their expressions of empathy may sometimes seem calculated or superficial.

6.3 Right and Wrong Through an ASPD Lens

6.3.1 How Individuals with ASPD View Rules and Laws

Many people with ASPD struggle with traditional moral frameworks. Their approach to right and wrong often depends on:

Personal Benefit: If following a rule benefits them, they may comply; if breaking a rule benefits them more, they may disregard it.

Risk and Consequence Analysis: Instead of feeling guilt, they may weigh the risks of punishment against the potential reward.

Control and Power: Some may view morality through the lens of control—those in power create the rules, and those who break them take power for themselves.

This perspective can make them highly strategic and pragmatic in decision-making, often prioritizing personal gain over conventional ethics.

6.3.2 The Gray Areas of Morality in ASPD

Not all individuals with ASPD see morality in absolute terms. Many function within society without engaging in criminal activity. Some even hold personal beliefs about fairness, loyalty, or justice—though these values are often based on logic rather than emotional conviction.

Examples of moral perspectives in ASPD include:

"Loyalty matters as long as it serves my interests."

"Cheating is only wrong if I get caught."

"Violence is justified if the other person deserves it."

These views demonstrate how moral reasoning in ASPD often prioritizes self-interest over traditional ethical considerations.

6.3.3 Can People with ASPD Be "Good"?

The definition of "good" depends on perspective. While individuals with ASPD may not experience morality in a conventional way, they can still:

Follow societal rules for pragmatic reasons.

Form personal ethical codes based on logic.

Engage in prosocial behavior when it aligns with their goals.

Some individuals with ASPD become successful businesspeople, leaders, or professionals who operate within legal and ethical boundaries—not because they feel obligated to do so, but because it benefits them.

Conclusion

Morality, empathy, and conscience are complex topics when viewed through the lens of ASPD. While individuals with the disorder often lack traditional emotional empathy and guilt, they are not inherently immoral or incapable of ethical behavior.

Instead, their approach to morality tends to be:

Pragmatic: Based on logic and self-interest rather than emotional conviction.

Strategic: Weighing risks and rewards rather than acting out of guilt or social obligation.

Individualized: Following personal moral codes rather than societal norms.

By understanding these differences, we can move beyond simplistic stereotypes and develop a more nuanced view of how individuals with ASPD navigate ethical and social landscapes.

◆Part 3:

The World's Response to ASPD

Chapter 7:

The Justice System and ASPD

Introduction

Antisocial Personality Disorder (ASPD) is often associated with criminal behavior, largely due to its defining characteristics of deceitfulness, impulsivity, and disregard for societal norms. However, the relationship between ASPD and criminality is complex and not as straightforward as it may seem. This chapter explores the intersection of ASPD and the justice system, questioning whether all criminals are antisocial and whether all individuals with ASPD engage in criminal activities. We will also examine the effectiveness of rehabilitation versus punishment and how the justice system often fails individuals with ASPD.

7.1 Are All Criminals Antisocial? Are All Antisocials Criminals?

7.1.1 Understanding Criminal Behavior and ASPD

While a significant proportion of individuals in the criminal justice system meet the criteria for ASPD, it is crucial to understand that not all criminals have ASPD, and not all people with ASPD are criminals. Criminal behavior can stem from various factors, including socio-economic conditions, mental health disorders other than ASPD, substance abuse, and environmental influences.

7.1.2 The Overrepresentation of ASPD in Criminal Populations

Studies estimate that approximately 50-80% of the prison population meets the diagnostic criteria for ASPD. This high percentage can be attributed to several factors:

Impulsivity: Individuals with ASPD often act without considering consequences, leading to impulsive crimes like theft, assault, or substance abuse.

Lack of Remorse: The absence of guilt or empathy can result in repeated criminal behavior, as there is no internal moral barrier preventing harmful actions.

Manipulative Tendencies: Individuals with ASPD may engage in fraud, scams, or other deceitful acts for personal gain.

However, the correlation between ASPD and criminality does not imply causation. Many individuals with ASPD never engage in illegal activities, finding alternative outlets for their tendencies, such as competitive careers, entrepreneurship, or high-risk sports.

7.1.3 ASPD Without Criminality

Not all individuals with ASPD engage in criminal behavior. Some exhibit antisocial traits in less conspicuous ways:

Corporate Misconduct: Engaging in unethical business practices that, while morally questionable, may not be illegal.

Interpersonal Manipulation: Exploiting personal relationships without breaking the law.

Legal but Unethical Actions: Finding loopholes or bending rules to benefit themselves without criminal consequences.

These individuals may never come into contact with the criminal justice system, but their behaviors still reflect the core traits of ASPD.

7.1.4 Criminals Without ASPD

Conversely, many criminals do not meet the diagnostic criteria for ASPD. Their actions may be motivated by:

Economic necessity: Engaging in illegal activities out of financial desperation.

Substance dependence: Committing crimes to support an addiction.

Acute stressors: Acting out in a moment of crisis without a history of antisocial behavior.

Understanding these distinctions is crucial for developing fair and effective justice system responses. Labeling all criminals as antisocial oversimplifies the complex motivations behind criminal behavior and risks unjustly stigmatizing individuals who do not fit the diagnostic criteria for ASPD.

7.1.5 The Role of Psychopathy

Psychopathy, a term often used interchangeably with ASPD, represents a more severe manifestation of antisocial behavior. While all psychopaths meet the criteria for ASPD, not all individuals with ASPD are psychopaths. Psychopathy is characterized by:

Shallow affect: Limited emotional response and inability to form deep emotional connections.

Callousness: Extreme lack of empathy and remorse.

Grandiosity: An inflated sense of self-importance.

Psychopaths are overrepresented in criminal populations, but like ASPD, psychopathy is not synonymous with criminality. Some psychopaths achieve success in fields like finance, politics, or entertainment, leveraging their traits for personal gain without engaging in illegal activities.

7.2 Rehabilitation vs. Punishment

7.2.1 The Punitive Approach

The justice system often adopts a punitive approach toward individuals with ASPD, focusing on punishment rather than rehabilitation. This is driven by the belief that individuals with ASPD are incapable of change, necessitating incarceration to protect society. Common punitive measures include:

Incarceration: Long prison sentences aimed at removing the individual from society.

Harsh penalties: Heavy fines, extended probation, or restrictive parole conditions.

Solitary confinement: Isolating the individual due to perceived threat or inability to integrate with the general prison population.

While these measures may serve as a temporary deterrent, they often fail to address the underlying issues that contribute to antisocial behavior.

7.2.2 The Limitations of Punishment

Punitive approaches have significant limitations when dealing with ASPD:

Recidivism: High rates of re-offending due to lack of rehabilitation or behavioral change.

Psychological deterioration: Prolonged incarceration can worsen antisocial traits, leading to increased aggression or emotional detachment.

Lack of treatment: Prisons rarely provide specialized therapy for ASPD, limiting opportunities for improvement.

Punishment alone does not address the neurological, psychological, and environmental factors that contribute to ASPD. Without intervention, individuals are likely to continue harmful behaviors upon release.

7.2.3 The Case for Rehabilitation

Rehabilitation offers a more holistic approach to addressing ASPD, focusing on behavioral change and social reintegration. Effective rehabilitation strategies include:

Cognitive Behavioral Therapy (CBT): Targeting maladaptive thought patterns and promoting healthier coping mechanisms.

Dialectical Behavioral Therapy (DBT): Emphasizing emotional regulation and interpersonal effectiveness.

Skill-building programs: Teaching vocational skills, conflict resolution, and anger management.

Rehabilitation recognizes that individuals with ASPD are not beyond help. With the right interventions, they can learn to manage their behaviors and reduce harmful actions.

7.2.4 Challenges in Rehabilitation

Despite its benefits, rehabilitation faces significant challenges:

Resistance to treatment: Individuals with ASPD may lack insight or motivation to change, hindering therapeutic progress.

Limited resources: Rehabilitation programs are often underfunded and understaffed, reducing their effectiveness.

Societal skepticism: Public perception that individuals with ASPD are "incurable" can lead to resistance against rehabilitative approaches.

However, case studies demonstrate that when properly implemented, rehabilitation can reduce recidivism and improve outcomes for individuals with ASPD.

7.2.5 Integrating Rehabilitation and Punishment

A balanced approach that combines punishment with rehabilitation may offer the most effective response to ASPD in the justice system. Potential strategies include:

Therapeutic communities within prisons: Creating environments where individuals can engage in therapy while serving their sentences.

Conditional parole: Offering early release based on participation in rehabilitative programs.

Post-release support: Providing access to ongoing therapy, employment assistance, and community resources.

By integrating rehabilitation with traditional punitive measures, the justice system can better address the complexities of ASPD and reduce harm to both individuals and society.

7.3 How the System Fails Those with ASPD

7.3.1 Misdiagnosis and Lack of Specialized Treatment

The justice system often fails to recognize and properly diagnose ASPD, resulting in inappropriate or ineffective treatment. Common issues include:

Misdiagnosis: Labeling individuals as "psychopaths" or "sociopaths" without formal assessment.

Lack of mental health screenings: Inadequate evaluation upon entry into the system.

Generic treatment plans: Using one-size-fits-all interventions that do not address the specific needs of individuals with ASPD.

Without accurate diagnosis and tailored treatment, the justice system cannot effectively address the root causes of antisocial behavior.

7.3.2 The Impact of Incarceration on ASPD

Incarceration can exacerbate antisocial traits, creating a cycle of offending and re-incarceration. Contributing factors include:

Exposure to violent environments: Prisons often foster aggression and criminal behavior.

Isolation: Solitary confinement can worsen emotional detachment and hostility.

Lack of social support: Limited access to family or community resources reduces opportunities for positive change.

Rather than serving as a corrective measure, incarceration often reinforces the behaviors that led to criminality in the first place.

7.3.3 Barriers to Reentry

Individuals with ASPD face significant challenges upon release from incarceration:

Employment discrimination: Difficulty finding work due to criminal records and stigma.

Social isolation: Struggles to rebuild relationships and reintegrate into the community.

Lack of mental health resources: Insufficient access to ongoing therapy or support services.

These barriers increase the risk of recidivism and hinder the individual's ability to build a stable, law-abiding life.

7.3.4 The Role of Probation and Parole

Probation and parole systems often fail to support individuals with ASPD effectively. Challenges include:

Strict conditions: Rules that are difficult for individuals with impulsivity and authority resistance to follow.

Punitive responses: Revoking parole for minor infractions rather than offering additional support.

Limited resources: Probation officers may lack training in handling ASPD or access to therapeutic resources.

A more rehabilitative approach to probation and parole could improve outcomes and reduce recidivism for individuals with ASPD.

7.3.5 Advocacy and Policy Reform

Addressing the failures of the justice system requires systemic change. Advocates and policymakers can:

Promote mental health screenings upon entry into the justice system.

Increase funding for rehabilitative programs tailored to ASPD.

Implement training for law enforcement, corrections officers, and parole officers on managing ASPD.

Encourage diversion programs that offer treatment instead of incarceration for non-violent offenders.

By adopting these reforms, the justice system can better support individuals with ASPD, reducing harm and promoting long-term change.

Conclusion

The intersection of ASPD and the justice system is fraught with challenges, from misdiagnosis and ineffective treatment to punitive approaches that fail to address the root causes of antisocial behavior. While not all criminals have ASPD, and not all individuals with ASPD engage in criminal activity, the justice system must evolve to recognize and address the complexities of this disorder.

Rehabilitation offers a promising alternative to punishment, emphasizing behavioral change and social reintegration. By combining rehabilitative approaches with targeted policy reforms, the justice system can better serve individuals with ASPD, reducing recidivism and promoting healthier, more productive lives.

Chapter 8:

Therapy, Treatment, and Management

Antisocial Personality Disorder (ASPD) has long been regarded as one of the most challenging personality disorders to treat. People diagnosed with ASPD often lack motivation to seek help, struggle with traditional therapeutic approaches, and experience difficulties forming trust-based relationships with mental health professionals. Additionally, many individuals with ASPD only enter treatment due to legal trouble, court-mandated programs, or external pressure rather than personal desire for change.

Despite these challenges, treatment and management are not entirely hopeless. While there is no "cure" for ASPD, certain approaches have shown promise in helping individuals improve impulse control, develop healthier coping mechanisms, and reduce harmful behaviors. This chapter explores the complexities of ASPD treatment, examines what works and what doesn't, and discusses strategies for leading a functional life with the disorder.

8.1 Can ASPD Be Treated?

One of the most debated questions in psychology and psychiatry is whether ASPD can truly be treated. The answer is complicated—while ASPD traits are deeply ingrained and resistant to change, some individuals have successfully learned to manage their behaviors and reduce the negative impact of their disorder.

8.1.1 The Challenges of Treating ASPD

Several factors make ASPD particularly difficult to treat:

Lack of Insight and Motivation: Many individuals with ASPD do not believe they have a problem or see a need for treatment. Unlike disorders such as anxiety or depression, where distress motivates people to seek help, those with ASPD often view their behavior as rational or even advantageous.

Manipulative Behavior: People with ASPD may use therapy sessions as an opportunity to manipulate therapists, feign progress, or exploit the system for personal gain.

Emotional Detachment: Traditional therapeutic methods rely on emotional processing, empathy-building, and trust—all of which can be difficult for someone with ASPD to engage in meaningfully.

High Dropout Rates: Many individuals with ASPD abandon treatment prematurely, particularly if they do not see immediate benefits or feel restricted by therapy.

Legal and External Pressures: Many individuals with ASPD only seek therapy after being mandated by a court, pressured by family, or required by a workplace. This external motivation often leads to minimal genuine engagement.

8.1.2 Why Some Believe ASPD is Untreatable

Due to the difficulties above, some mental health professionals believe ASPD is largely untreatable. The disorder's rigid behavioral patterns, resistance to authority, and emotional detachment make long-term success rare.

Additionally, traditional therapeutic methods—such as empathy training or deep emotional introspection—often fail to connect with individuals who lack the capacity for emotional engagement.

However, this does not mean that people with ASPD are beyond help. Rather, it suggests that treatment must be carefully tailored to their specific needs, strengths, and cognitive patterns rather than applying conventional approaches used for other mental disorders.

8.2 What Works (and What Doesn't)

Given the challenges, what therapeutic approaches have shown success in treating and managing ASPD? While there is no universal treatment, some methods have demonstrated effectiveness in modifying behavior, improving impulse control, and helping individuals function in society.

8.2.1 Ineffective or Controversial Approaches

Some traditional treatment approaches that work for other disorders tend to be ineffective or even counterproductive for ASPD:

Cognitive Behavioral Therapy (CBT): While CBT is effective for anxiety, depression, and other conditions, its impact on ASPD is limited. People with ASPD may struggle with self-reflection and empathy-building techniques central to CBT. However, structured CBT focused on behavioral modification may be useful.

Medication: Unlike mood disorders, where medication plays a crucial role, there is no specific drug that "treats" ASPD. Some medications, such as mood stabilizers or antipsychotics, may help control impulsivity or aggression, but they do not change core personality traits.

Empathy Training: Attempting to "teach" empathy to individuals with ASPD often fails, as their emotional detachment makes it difficult for them to internalize or genuinely experience emotions the way others do.

Psychoanalysis: Traditional psychoanalytic therapy, which focuses on deep emotional processing, childhood experiences, and unconscious motives, is often ineffective for ASPD because it requires a level of introspection many individuals with ASPD struggle with.

8.2.2 Effective Treatment Strategies

While some methods fail, others show promise in managing ASPD symptoms and improving overall functioning:

Behavioral Therapy (Contingency Management): This approach focuses on reinforcing positive behaviors and discouraging harmful ones. Reward systems, structured environments, and clear consequences for actions help guide behavioral change.

Group Therapy (Under Strict Conditions): While many with ASPD may manipulate group therapy settings, structured programs that emphasize accountability (such as 12-step programs or court-mandated groups) can sometimes encourage better social behavior.

Skills-Based Training: Instead of focusing on emotions, therapy for ASPD is often more effective when it teaches concrete skills—such as anger management, impulse control, problem-solving, and social strategies for personal gain without harming others.

Legal and Social Consequences: While not a therapy method, the presence of clear consequences—such as legal repercussions or career setbacks—can act as a deterrent, motivating individuals to modify their behavior to avoid punishment.

8.3 Building a Functional Life with ASPD

Even if ASPD cannot be "cured," individuals can still learn to build a structured and functional life. With the right strategies, some people with ASPD manage to hold jobs, maintain relationships, and avoid legal trouble.

8.3.1 Finding Motivation for Change

Because many individuals with ASPD lack internal motivation for self-improvement, the key to successful management is often linking change to personal benefit:

Career and Financial Stability: Learning to regulate behavior can help maintain employment and professional relationships.

Avoiding Legal Trouble: Managing impulsive or reckless behavior reduces the risk of incarceration.

Building Useful Relationships: Even if emotional connections are weak, understanding social rules can help form beneficial partnerships in business and personal life.

8.3.2 Managing Impulsivity and Aggression

Since impulsivity and aggression are core ASPD traits, individuals can benefit from strategies that focus on:

Recognizing Triggers: Identifying situations that provoke impulsive reactions.

Practicing Delayed Decision-Making: Teaching oneself to wait before making major decisions or reacting emotionally.

Using Logic Over Emotion: Reframing interactions in a logical way to minimize conflict.

8.3.3 Adapting to Social Norms Without Losing Independence

One of the biggest struggles for those with ASPD is navigating social norms while maintaining personal autonomy. Strategies for achieving this balance include:

Understanding Social Rules as Strategy: Instead of viewing social norms as constraints, individuals with ASPD can see them as useful tools for achieving personal and professional success.

Minimizing Conflict: Learning how to avoid unnecessary confrontations that could lead to personal loss.

Developing Functional Relationships: Even if emotional bonds are weak, maintaining cooperative relationships benefits long-term stability.

Conclusion

While ASPD is one of the most difficult personality disorders to treat, it is not entirely untreatable. The key lies in finding approaches that align with the cognitive patterns and motivations of individuals with ASPD rather than trying to impose traditional emotional therapies. While deep empathy or emotional transformation may be unrealistic, behavioral modification, impulse control strategies, and structured environments can help individuals with ASPD lead more functional and socially acceptable lives.

Although full recovery is unlikely, management is possible. With the right motivation, structure, and accountability, individuals with ASPD can navigate society successfully—minimizing harm to themselves and others while maximizing personal benefit.

◆ Part 4:

◆ Personal Stories and Perspectives

Chapter 9:

Voices from the Inside – Firsthand Accounts of ASPD

Understanding Antisocial Personality Disorder (ASPD) through clinical definitions and scientific studies only provides part of the picture. To truly grasp the reality of living with ASPD, it is essential to hear from those who experience it firsthand. While many individuals with ASPD do not seek out diagnosis or treatment, those who do often have unique insights into their thoughts, struggles, and personal growth.

This chapter presents a collection of firsthand accounts—some from real individuals (kept anonymous) and others fictionalized based on common experiences. These narratives provide a rare glimpse into how people with ASPD perceive themselves, their relationships, and society. While no two experiences are identical, common themes emerge: detachment, difficulty with trust, a strategic rather than emotional approach to relationships, and a strong focus on personal benefit.

9.1 Stories from Individuals with ASPD (Anonymous or Fictionalized)

Each individual with ASPD has a unique perspective. While some embrace their traits, others recognize the difficulties they create and attempt to adjust their behavior. Below are several narratives—some anonymized, others fictionalized based on common ASPD experiences.

9.1.1 The Strategic Businessman

"People think I'm cold. They say I don't care about anyone but myself. Maybe that's true, but I don't see the problem. The world is about power—who has it, who wants it, and who knows how to take it. I don't waste time on emotions. I get things done."

"I run a successful business. I know how to read people, figure out what they want, and use it to my advantage. That's not manipulation—it's just playing the game better than others. Do I have friends? Not really. I have useful connections. I don't waste time on people who can't help me in some way. And I don't lose sleep over my decisions. Business is business."

"Therapists say I lack empathy. Maybe. I see emotions as weaknesses. They cloud judgment. I don't need therapy—I need results. But if playing by the rules keeps my business running smoothly, I'll do it. It's all about the bigger picture."

9.1.2 The Charming Manipulator

"I know how to make people like me. It's easy—smile, say the right words, act like you care. People eat that up. They want to feel important, so I let them. If I need something, I know exactly what to say to get it."

"Some call it manipulation. I call it survival. Everyone plays a role in life. Some are sheep, some are wolves. I'm not going to apologize for knowing how to get what I want."

"I've been in and out of therapy. It's a joke. The therapists think they understand me, but they don't. They believe I need to 'connect' with people more. Why? So I can be like them? No thanks. I know how to function in society—I just do it my way."

9.1.3 The Self-Aware Outsider

"I know something is different about me. I don't react the way other people do. I don't feel bad when I hurt someone's feelings. I don't feel guilt, not in the way I've heard others describe it. I've learned to fake it because that's what's expected. But I don't really care."

"That doesn't mean I want to hurt people. I just don't care about the same things others do. I've studied human emotions like a scientist. I've figured out how to act 'normal' enough to fit in. It's exhausting, but it keeps me out of trouble."

"I've read about ASPD. I see myself in the descriptions. But I also see how society assumes we're all dangerous. I've never committed a crime. I hold a job. I live a normal life—just without the emotional complications most people seem to have."

9.2 Challenges, Successes, and Personal Growth

While ASPD comes with difficulties, not all individuals with the disorder experience life in the same way. Some struggle with authority and repeated legal trouble, while others channel their traits into highly successful careers.

9.2.1 The Struggles of Living with ASPD

Many individuals with ASPD face significant challenges in life, including:

Legal Issues: Due to impulsivity and disregard for rules, many individuals with ASPD find themselves entangled in legal trouble. This is especially true for those who engage in reckless or criminal behavior.

Relationship Difficulties: Maintaining close personal relationships is often challenging, as others may feel used, manipulated, or emotionally unfulfilled.

Lack of Fulfillment: Some individuals recognize that their way of thinking isolates them from deeper connections, leading to a sense of boredom or frustration.

Workplace Conflicts: While some thrive in competitive careers, others struggle with authority and structured environments.

9.2.2 Success Stories: When ASPD Traits Become an Advantage

Not everyone with ASPD experiences life as a constant struggle. Some manage to use their traits to their advantage, particularly in areas that reward strategic thinking, risk-taking, and emotional detachment.

Business and Leadership: Many high-powered executives display ASPD traits—confidence, decisiveness, and a lack of emotional attachment to tough decisions.

Law Enforcement and Military Careers: The ability to remain unemotional under pressure can be an asset in these fields.

Competitive Sports: The drive to win and lack of emotional distraction can make individuals with ASPD highly successful athletes.

Entrepreneurship: Risk-taking, strategic thinking, and a lack of emotional attachment to failure can help in starting and running businesses.

9.2.3 Can Personal Growth Happen with ASPD?

While personality disorders are generally stable over time, some individuals with ASPD do experience growth and adaptation. This is often due to:

Learning from Consequences: Repeated legal trouble or job losses may lead to behavioral adjustments.

Cognitive Awareness: Some individuals recognize the disadvantages of their traits and make conscious efforts to modify certain behaviors.

External Motivators: Financial stability, career advancement, or personal gain can drive some individuals to adopt socially acceptable behaviors.

9.3 How They See the World Differently

The unique worldview of someone with ASPD is often difficult for neurotypical individuals to understand. Their perception of relationships, morality, and society differs in fundamental ways.

9.3.1 Emotional Detachment and Logical Thinking

Many individuals with ASPD report feeling detached from emotions, leading to a more logical and calculated approach to decision-making.

"I don't let emotions cloud my judgment."

"Love? I see it as an exchange—people give because they expect something in return."

"Regret is pointless. Either you win or you learn."

9.3.2 A Different View on Morality

People with ASPD often see morality as relative rather than absolute.

"There's no such thing as 'right' or 'wrong.' There's what works and what doesn't."

"People follow rules because they're afraid of consequences. That's the only real reason."

"If I can get away with it, why not?"

9.3.3 Understanding Society as a Game

Many with ASPD see social interactions as a game—one with clear winners and losers.

"People are predictable. Learn their patterns, and you can control outcomes."

"Most people are ruled by emotions. That makes them easy to manipulate."

"I don't see the need for guilt. If I do something, it's because I decided to. Simple as that."

Conclusion

The firsthand experiences of individuals with ASPD reveal a complex and often misunderstood reality. While some embrace their traits, others struggle with the consequences. Some thrive in competitive environments, while others face legal and social difficulties.

Understanding ASPD from the inside challenges common stereotypes. Not all individuals with ASPD are criminals or incapable of change. Many learn to navigate society in ways that benefit them while minimizing harm to others.

Ultimately, these voices provide a glimpse into a world that operates by different rules—one where logic often outweighs emotion, and morality is a matter of perspective.

Chapter 10:

Living with Someone Who Has ASPD – Family & Friends Speak

Understanding the dynamics of living with someone who has Antisocial Personality Disorder (ASPD) is essential for family members, friends, and loved ones. This chapter delves into the unique challenges that arise when someone close to you is diagnosed with ASPD, and offers a perspective from both the individuals living with ASPD and their support systems. We will explore the psychological, emotional, and practical obstacles that family and friends face while offering insight on how to protect one's own mental health and maintain relationships despite these struggles.

10.1 The Challenges of Loving Someone with ASPD

Loving someone with ASPD can be a deeply complicated and emotionally exhausting experience. Often, family members and friends find themselves grappling with a blend of affection, frustration, and confusion, as the behaviors associated with ASPD can severely strain relationships.

    i.   Emotional Disconnection and Manipulation

Individuals with ASPD often exhibit a lack of emotional depth, which can make it incredibly difficult for loved ones to feel truly connected. People with ASPD typically do not engage in deep emotional exchanges, leading to feelings of emotional isolation in relationships. For family members, this lack of genuine emotional connection can feel like a constant struggle to "get through" to the individual. The manipulation of emotions becomes a core part of the dynamic, as individuals with ASPD may use charm or deceit to exploit loved ones for personal gain, making it even harder to trust them.

ii. Erosion of Trust and Respect

Trust and respect are pillars of healthy relationships, but these can be severely eroded when dealing with someone with ASPD. Lying, deceit, and a general disregard for others' feelings are frequent behaviors, which, over time, break down the foundation of trust. Family members or friends may find themselves in a constant state of doubt, never fully sure of what is true or who they can trust. This ongoing betrayal creates a hostile emotional environment and can have lasting consequences for relationships.

iii. The Strain on Family Dynamics

Relationships with individuals with ASPD often cause family dynamics to become strained. Siblings, parents, and other family members may experience feelings of resentment, hurt, and even guilt. The person with ASPD may disrupt family events or cause conflicts, either intentionally or because of their lack of empathy for the emotional well-being of others. Family members often face the difficult decision of whether to cut ties with the individual or continue trying to support them, even when it feels like no progress is being made.

10.2 Setting Boundaries and Protecting Your Mental Health

It is crucial for individuals who are living with someone who has ASPD to establish clear and firm boundaries in order to protect their own mental health. Boundaries are essential in any relationship but become even more important when interacting with someone who exhibits manipulative or harmful behaviors due to ASPD.

i. Establishing Healthy Boundaries

Boundaries help define the space in which you feel safe, both emotionally and physically. Setting boundaries with someone who has ASPD may involve clear limits on what is acceptable behavior and what is not. For example, family members may need to enforce strict rules about honesty, respectful communication, or involvement in personal matters. These boundaries act as safeguards to ensure that individuals with ASPD cannot exploit or take advantage of loved ones.

ii. Recognizing When to Walk Away

Sometimes, despite best efforts, a relationship with someone who has ASPD may become too toxic or dangerous to maintain. It is crucial to recognize when walking away is the healthiest choice for both yourself and the individual with ASPD. Family members and friends may struggle with feelings of guilt or shame when deciding to sever ties, but it's important to understand that putting your own mental and emotional well-being first is necessary. In extreme cases, continued exposure to the individual's harmful behavior can lead to depression, anxiety, or emotional burnout.

iii. Seeking External Support

One of the most beneficial steps loved ones can take when living with someone who has ASPD is seeking professional help or counseling. Therapy, support groups, and even legal advice can provide vital resources for understanding the dynamics of the relationship and establishing strategies for coping. Group therapy or counseling with the person with ASPD can sometimes help establish better communication and improve behavior patterns, but only if the individual with ASPD is willing to participate in the process.

10.3 Can Relationships with Someone with ASPD Work?

A question often posed by those living with someone who has ASPD is whether it is possible for relationships to thrive or even survive. While it can be difficult, there are instances where relationships may work, but it requires intense effort, a high degree of self-awareness, and realistic expectations.

i. The Role of Therapy and Treatment

For relationships to work, therapy or counseling is often a necessity. Therapy for the individual with ASPD, especially if they are willing to participate, can lead to better coping mechanisms and a reduction in harmful behaviors. While therapy may not "cure" ASPD, it can help individuals with the disorder develop strategies for managing impulsive actions and improving their interactions with others. In cases where both parties in the relationship are committed to understanding the disorder and working toward resolution, positive changes can be achieved.

ii. Unrealistic Expectations and Reality

It is important for both parties to have realistic expectations about what a relationship with someone who has ASPD will look like. Emotional highs and lows, manipulation, and a lack of empathy will likely be part of the dynamic. However, with the right boundaries, support systems, and understanding, relationships can sometimes evolve into functional, albeit non-traditional, arrangements. Loved ones must come to terms with the fact that they may not get the emotional fulfillment they would normally expect from a relationship, but this does not mean the relationship is without value.

iii. The Importance of Self-Care

While maintaining a relationship with someone who has ASPD can be challenging, self-care is a fundamental element to ensure that the individual is not overwhelmed by the emotional toll. Engaging in hobbies, spending time with supportive friends and family, and taking time for self-reflection are all essential activities for maintaining one's mental health. Practicing self-care allows the person who is supporting the individual with ASPD to feel empowered and equipped to handle the emotional challenges of the relationship.

◆Part 5:

◆Deeper Psychological and Social Exploration

Chapter 11:

The Spectrum of Antisocial Traits

Antisocial Personality Disorder (ASPD) is not a monolithic condition. The expression of ASPD varies significantly between individuals, and understanding its spectrum is critical for both diagnosis and treatment. Not all cases of ASPD are the same, and the traits associated with the disorder can manifest in ways that range from subtle, high-functioning behaviors to more overt, low-functioning actions. This chapter examines these differences, explores the continuum of ASPD traits, and delves into the complexities of distinguishing between "ruthless" behavior and the characteristics of a disordered personality.

11.1 Not All ASPD Cases Are the Same

ASPD is a spectrum disorder, meaning that individuals with the condition can experience varying degrees of severity. The traits associated with ASPD can present differently in each person, which makes the disorder particularly difficult to generalize. While some people may exhibit extreme manifestations of antisocial behavior, others may appear more "normal" in their day-to-day functioning.

i. The Spectrum of Antisocial Traits

ASPD is characterized by a persistent pattern of disregard for the rights of others, but this core feature can manifest in various ways. For example, some individuals with ASPD may engage in criminal or violent behavior, while others may exhibit more subtle forms of manipulation or exploitation. The severity of these behaviors often depends on the individual's level of functioning, personal circumstances, and environment.

Mild ASPD Traits: In some cases, individuals may demonstrate characteristics of ASPD, such as dishonesty or impulsivity, but may not engage in criminal activities or violent behavior. These individuals might still have difficulty forming meaningful connections and may manipulate others for personal gain, but their actions are typically less extreme.

Moderate ASPD Traits: Those with moderate ASPD traits might engage in occasional illegal activities or exploit others for personal benefit. They may be skilled at manipulating others emotionally, though their behaviors are often still within the confines of societal expectations in some contexts. These individuals may function well in certain social situations, but their relationships tend to be shallow and self-serving.

Severe ASPD Traits: At the extreme end of the spectrum, individuals with severe ASPD traits might exhibit violent tendencies, criminal behavior, or a complete disregard for the well-being of others. These individuals often struggle to form relationships and may have a history of legal issues or substance abuse. They may feel little to no empathy for others, and their actions may be impulsive and harmful.

ii.   Factors Influencing ASPD Expression

Several factors can influence how ASPD manifests in an individual. Genetics, environmental stressors, childhood trauma, and social upbringing all contribute to how antisocial traits develop and evolve. For example, a person who grows up in an abusive or neglectful environment may develop more extreme forms of ASPD traits due to early maladaptive coping mechanisms. On the other hand, an individual who experiences less severe environmental stressors may develop milder forms of the disorder.

Genetics and Biology: Studies suggest that ASPD may have a genetic component, with some individuals being predisposed to antisocial traits due to inherited characteristics. Brain abnormalities, such as deficits in the prefrontal cortex (which is involved in decision-making and impulse control), may also contribute to the expression of ASPD.

Environment and Upbringing: A traumatic or neglectful childhood can increase the risk of developing ASPD. Exposure to violence, substance abuse, or parental neglect may make individuals more likely to develop the traits associated with the disorder. Conversely, a stable and nurturing environment may help mitigate the severity of ASPD traits.

11.2 High-Functioning vs. Low-Functioning ASPD

A key distinction within ASPD is the difference between high-functioning and low-functioning individuals. These terms are used to describe the degree to which an individual with ASPD is able to maintain their daily life, relationships, and societal roles.

i. High-Functioning ASPD

High-functioning individuals with ASPD are often able to maintain a semblance of normalcy in their lives. They may hold down jobs, have families, and engage in social activities without drawing attention to their antisocial traits. These individuals are typically skilled at masking their behaviors and may use charm, intelligence, or manipulation to navigate social situations.

Superficial Charm: High-functioning individuals with ASPD are often charismatic and able to charm others. They may appear friendly, confident, and socially adept, which can mask their underlying disregard for others. This charm may help them gain the trust of others and exploit their relationships for personal gain.

Success in Careers and Social Situations: Many high-functioning individuals with ASPD are able to excel in their careers, particularly in competitive fields where manipulation, risk-taking, and self-interest are advantageous. These individuals may thrive in environments that reward assertiveness and decisiveness, using their manipulative skills to climb the social or corporate ladder.

Emotional Detachment: Despite their outward success, high-functioning individuals with ASPD often struggle with emotional detachment. While they may be able to form superficial relationships, they typically lack empathy and the ability to connect with others on a deep emotional level. This emotional emptiness can leave them feeling isolated, even if they are surrounded by people.

ii. Low-Functioning ASPD

On the other end of the spectrum, low-functioning individuals with ASPD may struggle significantly with basic life tasks. They may have a history of legal issues, substance abuse, or unstable relationships. Their antisocial behaviors are often more apparent and more disruptive, leading to difficulties in maintaining employment, relationships, and daily responsibilities.

Criminal Behavior and Legal Issues: Low-functioning individuals with ASPD are more likely to engage in criminal behavior, ranging from theft to violent crime. These individuals may have a history of arrests, incarceration, and a general disregard for societal laws and norms.

Impulsive and Self-Destructive Tendencies: Individuals with low-functioning ASPD may engage in impulsive or reckless behaviors that put themselves and others at risk. These individuals often lack impulse control, which can lead to substance abuse, violence, or other risky activities. Their actions may be reactive rather than planned, and they may struggle to understand or control their behavior.

Difficulty with Relationships: Low-functioning individuals with ASPD often experience deep difficulties in forming and maintaining relationships. Their lack of empathy, combined with their impulsivity and aggression, makes it difficult for them to connect with others in a meaningful way. These individuals may burn bridges with family members, friends, and coworkers due to their erratic and harmful behavior.

11.3 Where Do You Draw the Line Between "Ruthless" and "Disordered"?

One of the most challenging aspects of ASPD is distinguishing between "ruthless" behavior and true personality disorder traits. In many cases, individuals with ASPD may display behaviors that are often seen as ruthless or callous, but these traits may not always signify a disordered personality. The line between a morally questionable individual and someone with a clinical personality disorder can be difficult to draw, and this raises important questions about how we define and treat antisocial behavior.

i. Ruthlessness vs. Maladaptive Traits

Some individuals may engage in ruthless behaviors, such as using others for personal gain or exhibiting a lack of compassion, without necessarily meeting the full criteria for ASPD. Ruthlessness, in this context, refers to a pattern of cold, calculated, and self-serving behavior, but it may not always stem from a personality disorder. In contrast, ASPD is characterized by pervasive patterns of disregard for others' rights, which are more ingrained and affect multiple areas of life, including relationships, work, and personal conduct.

ii. The Role of Environment and Choice

In some cases, environmental factors or personal choices may drive behavior that appears to be characteristic of ASPD, even if the individual does not meet the clinical criteria. For example, someone who grows up in a highly competitive environment may develop traits that mimic those of ASPD, such as manipulation or exploitation, but this may be a learned behavior rather than a result of a disordered personality.

iii. Diagnosis and Criteria for ASPD

To be diagnosed with ASPD, an individual must exhibit a consistent pattern of behavior that includes a lack of empathy, manipulation, deceit, and impulsivity. A trained mental health professional will assess the individual's behavior over time and across various situations to determine if they meet the criteria for ASPD. The key difference between someone who is ruthless and someone with ASPD is the persistent, pervasive nature of the behavior and the inability to change without therapeutic intervention.

Chapter 12:

The Role of Society in Shaping Antisocial Behavior

Antisocial behavior does not emerge in a vacuum. It is heavily influenced by various factors within the broader societal context, such as the environment, upbringing, exposure to trauma, and social norms. Understanding the role society plays in shaping antisocial behavior is critical to comprehending how individuals with Antisocial Personality Disorder (ASPD) develop their traits. Moreover, examining how society can either exacerbate or mitigate these tendencies will shed light on the broader implications of prevention, intervention, and treatment strategies.

12.1 How Environment Influences Antisocial Traits

The environment in which an individual is raised plays a pivotal role in the development of antisocial traits. From childhood through adulthood, an individual's exposure to different social, economic, and cultural environments can either contribute to or alleviate the potential for antisocial behavior.

i. Family Environment

The family is often the first and most influential environment in which a child develops. A supportive and nurturing family environment can provide emotional stability, positive role models, and a sense of belonging. In contrast, a dysfunctional or neglectful family can contribute to the development of antisocial traits. Studies have shown that children who grow up in households characterized by abuse, neglect, or inconsistent parenting are more likely to exhibit conduct problems and later develop ASPD.

Abuse and Neglect: Children who experience physical, emotional, or sexual abuse are at a significantly higher risk of developing antisocial traits. The trauma caused by abuse often leads to a distorted view of the world, where the individual learns to distrust others, manipulate situations, and suppress emotions as a form of self-protection. Additionally, neglect, where emotional or physical needs are not adequately met, can leave a child feeling abandoned and unworthy, which may foster feelings of anger, resentment, and disregard for others.

Inconsistent Parenting: A family dynamic characterized by inconsistent discipline, where the child experiences extreme punishments or lack of boundaries, can create confusion and resentment. The child may fail to learn empathy or develop healthy coping mechanisms for dealing with frustration and disappointment. In these households, children may grow up without a clear understanding of right and wrong, leading to difficulties in forming meaningful relationships and establishing a moral compass.

ii. Peer Influences and Socialization

As children and adolescents grow older, the role of peers and social circles becomes increasingly important. Adolescents, in particular, are highly impressionable and may adopt behaviors modeled by their peers. If a child is surrounded by peers who engage in antisocial or criminal activities, they may begin to see such behavior as normal and even rewarding.

Peer Pressure: Peer pressure can play a significant role in shaping antisocial behavior. If a young person is part of a group that encourages or rewards rebellious behavior, they may be more likely to engage in activities like bullying, cheating, stealing, or violence. Peer groups can reinforce these behaviors, making it more difficult for the individual to develop empathy or understand the consequences of their actions.

Gang Membership: In some cases, the environment can include more formal groups, such as gangs, which explicitly promote antisocial behavior as part of their identity. Gang members often engage in criminal activities, and the need for belonging can overshadow any moral concerns. The sense of power, loyalty, and protection that gangs offer can further entrench antisocial behavior in vulnerable individuals.

iii. Community Environment

The broader community in which an individual lives can also influence the development of antisocial traits. Areas with high levels of poverty, violence, and crime can shape how a person interacts with the world and develops coping mechanisms. In communities with limited resources or opportunities, individuals may be more inclined to engage in antisocial or criminal behavior as a means of survival or gaining social status.

Social Inequality: Communities characterized by economic disparity, lack of education, and unemployment often create an environment where antisocial behavior can thrive. In such communities, individuals may feel that they have fewer opportunities for success through conventional means and turn to illegal activities to attain material goods or social status. Additionally, the lack of social cohesion and trust within these communities can foster a sense of isolation and hostility toward others, which are key components of ASPD.

Exposure to Violence: Children and adolescents who grow up in violent neighborhoods may be desensitized to violence and develop a distorted sense of morality. Constant exposure to aggression, crime, and drug use can normalize antisocial behavior, making it harder for individuals to empathize with others or understand the consequences of their actions. In some cases, individuals may adopt violence as a way to exert power or control in their own lives, perpetuating the cycle of antisocial behavior.

12.2 The Role of Trauma, Neglect, and Upbringing

Trauma and neglect are among the most significant contributors to the development of antisocial traits. The experiences individuals have in early life can leave lasting emotional scars that shape their views on relationships, trust, and personal worth.

i. Childhood Trauma

Early experiences of trauma can dramatically alter a child's emotional development and perception of the world. Traumatic experiences, such as physical or sexual abuse, witnessing violence, or experiencing the death of a caregiver, can distort how a child perceives their environment. For some, these early adversities lead to an inability to trust others, which is a core feature of ASPD.

Physical Abuse: Children who are physically abused may develop a defensive, combative stance toward the world. They may believe that in order to survive, they must be aggressive and dominant, pushing aside feelings of vulnerability or dependence on others. The inability to trust caregivers or authority figures can prevent these children from learning appropriate social and emotional responses, contributing to the development of antisocial behaviors later in life.

Sexual Abuse: Sexual abuse can have profound effects on a child's emotional health. In many cases, children who experience sexual abuse may grow up with a distorted sense of self-worth and an unhealthy understanding of relationships. The shame and guilt associated with sexual trauma can lead individuals to develop maladaptive coping strategies, such as emotional numbness, manipulation, or detachment.

ii. Neglect and Emotional Deprivation

Neglect, where a child's basic emotional or physical needs are unmet, can leave profound psychological scars. Neglect may occur when caregivers fail to provide proper nutrition, supervision, love, or attention. Children who experience neglect may grow up feeling unloved, unwanted, and unimportant, which can lead to difficulties in forming healthy attachments and an inability to empathize with others.

Emotional Neglect: Emotional neglect occurs when caregivers fail to respond to a child's emotional needs, leading to a sense of emotional isolation. This neglect may prevent the child from developing a strong sense of self-worth or healthy emotional regulation, resulting in the development of antisocial traits, such as coldness, manipulation, and emotional detachment.

Lack of Boundaries: In households where neglect is prevalent, children may never learn proper boundaries, both with others and themselves. Without the guidance of caregivers, they may struggle to understand concepts like respect, personal space, and reciprocity in relationships. This lack of boundary setting can lead to exploitative behaviors and an inability to recognize the rights of others.

12.3 Can Society Create More Antisocial People?

The question of whether society plays a direct role in creating antisocial individuals is a controversial one, but there are undeniable links between societal structures and the prevalence of antisocial behavior. While individuals may be predisposed to certain antisocial traits through genetic or environmental factors, societal conditions can either foster or mitigate these behaviors.

i. Media Influence

Society's portrayal of antisocial behavior in the media can significantly impact how people view and act on antisocial traits. Violence, manipulation, and disregard for authority are often glamorized in movies, television shows, and video games, making these behaviors appear heroic, desirable, or even justified.

Violence in the Media: The normalization of violence in the media can desensitize individuals to the real-life consequences of violent behavior. When violence is glorified or depicted as a solution to problems, individuals—especially young, impressionable viewers—may begin to adopt these behaviors as acceptable ways to resolve conflicts or assert control.

Antiheroes and Role Models: The popularity of antiheroes in modern media—characters who break the rules, manipulate others, and operate outside societal norms—may contribute to the glamorization of antisocial behavior. These characters often get what they want, reinforcing the idea that manipulating, deceiving, and disregarding others' rights is an effective way to succeed in life.

ii. Cultural Norms and Values

Cultural norms and values play a significant role in shaping an individual's behavior. In societies that emphasize competition, individualism, and material success, individuals may feel pressured to adopt antisocial traits to succeed. When personal gain is prioritized over collective well-being, antisocial behavior may be viewed as a necessary evil or even a desirable trait.

Capitalism and Social Darwinism: In highly competitive societies, individuals may be taught that success is a result of personal effort and the ability to outperform others. This mindset can create a culture in which exploiting, deceiving, or stepping on others is seen as acceptable or even necessary for survival. Individuals who prioritize their personal goals above the needs of others may be more likely to develop antisocial traits.

Individualism vs. Collectivism: In cultures where individualism is highly valued, there may be less emphasis on empathy, cooperation, and shared responsibility. In such environments, individuals may be more likely to view others as tools to be used for personal gain rather than as people with inherent value and rights.

iii. Economic and Social Structures

Economic inequality, lack of access to education, and poor social services can contribute to the development of antisocial traits. In societies with vast economic disparities, individuals who feel disenfranchised or excluded may turn to antisocial behavior as a means of coping or achieving success.

Poverty and Crime: Poverty can create an environment where crime is more likely to be seen as an opportunity rather than a moral failing. When individuals lack access to basic resources such as healthcare, education, and housing, they may resort to antisocial behaviors, such as theft or fraud, to survive.

Incarceration and Stigmatization: Societal responses to crime, particularly through mass incarceration, can exacerbate antisocial traits. Rather than providing opportunities for rehabilitation, the criminal justice system often reinforces antisocial behavior by stigmatizing offenders and offering limited resources for reintegration into society.

Conclusion: Society plays a crucial role in shaping antisocial behavior, both by contributing to the environment in which individuals develop and by either supporting or undermining the development of healthier behaviors. Environmental factors such as family life, peer influences, and community norms can either foster or prevent the emergence of antisocial traits. Additionally, societal structures that emphasize competition, material success, and individualism can contribute to the growth of antisocial behavior. A deeper understanding of these influences is essential to addressing the root causes of ASPD and creating a society where empathy, compassion, and collaboration are valued over exploitation and manipulation.

Chapter 13:

The Dark Side of Charisma – When ASPD Becomes an Advantage

Antisocial Personality Disorder (ASPD) is often associated with negative traits such as manipulation, lack of empathy, and disregard for social norms. However, in certain environments, individuals with ASPD may use these same characteristics to their advantage, often thriving in competitive settings where ruthlessness and a disregard for others can lead to success. This chapter explores the darker side of ASPD, where traits such as charisma, confidence, and assertiveness are strategically used to ascend in business, leadership, and power dynamics. It also delves into the ethical considerations of power and manipulation, questioning whether the ends justify the means.

13.1 Leadership, Business, and Power – The "Successful" Side of ASPD

While many view ASPD traits as inherently problematic, certain characteristics associated with the disorder can be seen as assets in leadership and business environments. The ability to remain unemotional, make tough decisions without hesitation, and manipulate social dynamics can be valuable in contexts where power and success are paramount.

    i.   Charisma and Confidence

One of the most striking traits of individuals with ASPD is their ability to exude confidence and charisma, often drawing others in with their magnetic personalities. These individuals may not exhibit typical signs of empathy, but they know how to captivate others, commanding respect and admiration without necessarily forming emotional connections.

Self-Assurance and Charm: Many individuals with ASPD are highly skilled at reading social situations and adjusting their behavior to fit the needs of the moment. This adaptability allows them to present themselves in a way that appeals to others, even if their motivations are self-serving. They may be perceived as confident and competent, qualities that are highly valued in leadership and business contexts.

Winning Trust: A person with ASPD may use their charm to win the trust of others, allowing them to position themselves in advantageous situations. They can manipulate social interactions to create a perception of competence and reliability, even if these traits do not reflect their true intentions. This ability to deceive, when used strategically, can open doors to business opportunities, leadership roles, and influential positions.

ii. Ruthlessness in Decision-Making

One of the key traits associated with ASPD is a lack of emotional attachment or empathy, which can allow individuals with the disorder to make decisions without being swayed by feelings of guilt or compassion. In business and leadership, this trait can be an asset, particularly in high-pressure environments where decisions must be made quickly and with little regard for the emotional impact on others.

Cutthroat Competitiveness: In competitive environments, individuals with ASPD may excel due to their willingness to make tough, often morally ambiguous decisions. They may not hesitate to make choices that benefit them personally, even if it means stepping on others or exploiting vulnerable individuals. In business, this type of behavior can lead to significant financial or professional gains, particularly when competition is fierce.

Risk-Taking and Innovation: People with ASPD are often unafraid of taking risks, even when the potential for failure is high. This boldness can be an asset in business, particularly in industries that reward innovation or risk-taking. The fearlessness to go against the grain or challenge established norms can lead to breakthroughs, although the underlying motivations may be driven by personal gain rather than a desire for the greater good.

iii. Ambition and Goal-Oriented Focus

Many individuals with ASPD possess an intense drive to achieve success, which can make them highly goal-oriented and motivated to climb the social or corporate ladder. This ambition can serve as a powerful tool, especially in environments where personal success is highly valued.

Relentless Pursuit of Success: Driven by an insatiable desire for power, wealth, and status, individuals with ASPD will stop at nothing to achieve their goals. They may use any means necessary to get ahead, including manipulation, deceit, and coercion. In environments where success is often the result of ruthless competition, this drive can lead to exceptional achievements.

Competitive Edge: The intense focus on success and power can provide individuals with ASPD a significant edge in competitive fields, such as business, politics, or entertainment. While their lack of empathy and willingness to deceive may be seen as unethical by some, these qualities can be advantageous in environments where winning is prioritized above all else.

13.2 How Some with ASPD Thrive in Competitive Environments

Certain environments, especially those that emphasize individual achievement and competition, can provide a fertile ground for individuals with ASPD to thrive. The qualities that typically make someone with ASPD a "problematic" member of society—such as manipulation, assertiveness, and a lack of empathy—can be used strategically to gain power and influence.

i. High-Stakes Professions and Industries

Some industries are particularly conducive to the success of individuals with ASPD traits. High-stakes fields such as finance, law, and politics often reward assertiveness, manipulation, and a cutthroat attitude, allowing those with ASPD to flourish in ways that others might find difficult.

Corporate World: In large corporate structures, individuals with ASPD may rise quickly through the ranks, using manipulation and strategic alliances to secure promotions and power. Their ability to make tough decisions without emotional baggage can make them appear decisive and capable, even if their choices are often self-serving or unethical.

Financial Markets: The financial sector, particularly in investment banking or hedge funds, can be a lucrative environment for individuals with ASPD traits. The desire for profit, the lack of moral constraints, and the ability to manipulate market dynamics can lead to significant financial success. Those with ASPD may excel in situations where others might hesitate due to ethical concerns, allowing them to take bold risks and reap the rewards.

ii. Political Power and Influence

In politics, individuals with ASPD may use their charisma, strategic thinking, and willingness to manipulate others to gain power. Political systems, especially in competitive environments, often reward those who can navigate complex power dynamics, form alliances, and ruthlessly pursue their objectives.

Strategic Manipulation: Politicians with ASPD traits are often adept at reading the political landscape and using information to their advantage. By cultivating a network of supporters and strategically eliminating opponents, they can rise to influential positions of power. Their ability to manipulate public opinion and project an image of competence can lead to widespread support, even if their actions are driven by selfish motivations.

Undermining Rivals: In the cutthroat world of politics, individuals with ASPD are often unafraid to use any means necessary to discredit or undermine their rivals. They may engage in smear campaigns, use blackmail, or exploit weaknesses in their opponents to secure a political advantage. In this environment, ruthlessness and manipulation can be assets, leading to significant political success.

iii. The Media and Entertainment Industry

The entertainment industry, like business and politics, rewards individuals who can command attention, manipulate public perception, and navigate complex social dynamics. Individuals with ASPD traits may thrive in this environment, using their charisma and strategic thinking to gain fame and influence.

Self-Promotion and Image Control: In the media and entertainment world, creating a compelling public persona is crucial to success. Individuals with ASPD are often skilled at self-promotion, cultivating an image that appeals to the public while hiding their true motivations. This ability to control their image and manipulate public perception can lead to immense popularity and career success.

Exploiting Others: The entertainment industry also provides opportunities for individuals with ASPD to exploit others. Whether through manipulation, coercion, or using others for personal gain, those with ASPD traits may take advantage of vulnerable individuals to further their own careers. The lack of empathy and disregard for the well-being of others allows them to climb the ladder without concern for the impact on those around them.

13.3 The Ethics of Power and Manipulation

While the traits associated with ASPD can be advantageous in certain environments, they raise significant ethical questions. The use of manipulation, deceit, and exploitation to achieve success often comes at the expense of others, and the line between strategic thinking and unethical behavior can be thin.

i. The Ends Justify the Means?

One of the central ethical dilemmas posed by individuals with ASPD is the question of whether the ends justify the means. In environments where success is highly valued, some may argue that achieving one's goals, even through morally questionable tactics, is acceptable as long as it leads to positive outcomes.

Moral Relativism: Individuals with ASPD often operate within a framework of moral relativism, where they do not adhere to universal ethical standards. Instead, they view their actions through a pragmatic lens, focusing on the outcome rather than the morality of the process. This perspective can make it difficult to judge their actions, as they may be seen as "successful" or "effective," regardless of the harm caused to others.

Manipulation for a Greater Good?: In some cases, individuals with ASPD may justify their manipulative behavior by arguing that their actions are for a greater good. They may view their success as a means of achieving societal or personal goals, even if their behavior is harmful to others. This rationalization raises complex questions about whether manipulation and deceit are acceptable if they lead to desirable outcomes.

ii. The Moral Cost of Success

While individuals with ASPD may achieve significant success in certain fields, the ethical cost of their behavior is high. Manipulating others, exploiting weaknesses, and engaging in deceitful practices can create a toxic environment for those around them. Over time, the accumulation of these moral compromises can take a toll on both the individual and the people they interact with.

Alienation and Isolation: The lack of empathy and disregard for others' feelings can lead to long-term isolation for individuals with ASPD. While they may achieve success in the short term, their relationships with others are often shallow, transactional, and self-serving. The pursuit of success at any cost can leave them without meaningful personal connections, ultimately undermining the very success they sought to achieve.

Cycle of Exploitation: As individuals with ASPD continue to manipulate and exploit others, they may find themselves caught in a cycle of exploitation. Their relationships are often one-sided, with little genuine emotional connection or reciprocity. This can lead to a lack of fulfillment and a growing sense of emptiness, as their success comes at the expense of their own humanity.

Conclusion: While Antisocial Personality Disorder is often viewed negatively due to its association with manipulation, deceit, and lack of empathy, it is clear that certain traits associated with the disorder can be leveraged for success in competitive environments. Charisma, confidence, ruthlessness, and a relentless drive for achievement can help individuals with ASPD thrive in business, politics, and entertainment. However, these advantages often come at a significant moral cost, raising important ethical questions about the nature of success, manipulation, and the value of human connection.

◆Part 6:

◆ Practical Guidance and Support

Chapter 14:

If You Think You Might Have ASPD... What Now?

Many people who read about Antisocial Personality Disorder (ASPD) begin to wonder if they might fit the criteria. Maybe you recognize some of the traits in yourself—manipulativeness, lack of empathy, impulsivity, or a disregard for rules. Perhaps others have accused you of being "cold," "uncaring," or even a "sociopath." But does that mean you have ASPD? What does a diagnosis mean, and is it even worth seeking one? More importantly, if you do have ASPD, how do you navigate relationships, work, and daily life in a world that may not understand you?

This chapter explores these questions in depth.

14.1 Signs That You Might Have ASPD

The first step in understanding whether you might have ASPD is to assess whether you display the core traits of the disorder. While only a mental health professional can provide an official diagnosis, self-reflection can be a useful starting point.

i. Recognizing the Core Symptoms

According to the DSM-5 (Diagnostic and Statistical Manual of Mental Disorders, Fifth Edition), ASPD is characterized by a persistent pattern of disregard for others' rights, beginning in childhood or adolescence and continuing into adulthood. Some of the primary symptoms include:

Disregard for laws and social norms – Engaging in behaviors that are illegal or socially unacceptable without concern for consequences.

Deceitfulness and manipulation – Frequently lying, conning others for personal gain, or using charm to manipulate situations.

Impulsivity – Acting without thinking, often leading to poor decision-making.

Irritability and aggressiveness – Getting into physical fights or displaying a quick temper.

Lack of remorse – Feeling little to no guilt for harming others, whether emotionally, financially, or physically.

Irresponsibility – Failing to meet work obligations, financial commitments, or personal responsibilities.

If these traits resonate with you, it may be worth exploring whether ASPD is a factor in your life.

ii.   Differentiating ASPD from Similar Traits

Just because someone is manipulative, impulsive, or emotionally detached does not automatically mean they have ASPD. Many people can be self-serving, aggressive, or even deceitful under certain circumstances, but they still function within the boundaries of social norms.

Key distinctions include:

Context matters – If your behavior is persistent across different situations (work, relationships, social settings), it is more indicative of ASPD.

Severity and impact – Many people occasionally act recklessly or break rules, but for those with ASPD, these behaviors are deeply ingrained and often lead to legal, financial, or interpersonal problems.

Lack of emotional connection – Individuals with ASPD often struggle to form genuine emotional bonds, even with close family and friends.

    iii.   Childhood Signs and Conduct Disorder

For an adult to be diagnosed with ASPD, there must be evidence of conduct disorder before the age of 15. Conduct disorder includes behaviors such as:

Repeated aggression toward people or animals

Destruction of property

Deceitfulness, lying, or stealing

Serious rule violations (running away, truancy, breaking curfews)

If these behaviors were present in your early life, it may further indicate a pattern consistent with ASPD.

14.2 Seeking a Diagnosis (Or Deciding Not To)

Not everyone who suspects they have ASPD will seek a formal diagnosis, and for good reason. Being officially diagnosed with ASPD can carry certain risks, including social stigma and potential legal implications.

i. The Benefits of a Diagnosis

For some, getting diagnosed can be helpful for several reasons:

Understanding Yourself – A diagnosis can provide clarity about why you think and act the way you do.

Access to Treatment – While ASPD is difficult to treat, certain therapies (such as cognitive behavioral therapy) can help with specific challenges like impulse control or emotional regulation.

Legal and Medical Documentation – If ASPD significantly impacts your ability to function, having a formal diagnosis may be useful for legal protections or medical treatment.

ii. The Risks of a Diagnosis

On the other hand, receiving an official ASPD diagnosis can come with downsides:

Stigma and Misunderstanding – Many people, including medical professionals, hold misconceptions about ASPD, which could lead to negative treatment.

Legal Consequences – A documented ASPD diagnosis could be used against you in legal situations, custody battles, or employment screenings.

Limited Treatment Options – Unlike disorders such as depression or anxiety, ASPD has no standard medical treatment, making some question the value of an official diagnosis.

iii. Self-Diagnosis vs. Professional Assessment

If you suspect you have ASPD but are hesitant to pursue a formal diagnosis, self-awareness can still be valuable. Reflecting on your behaviors and their impact on others can help you make better decisions, even without a clinical label.

However, if you are struggling with severe impulsivity, frequent legal trouble, or difficulty maintaining relationships, speaking with a mental health professional may be beneficial.

14.3 Managing Relationships, Work, and Daily Life

Whether or not you seek a diagnosis, managing the challenges that come with ASPD is essential for leading a functional life.

i. Navigating Relationships

People with ASPD often struggle with relationships due to their difficulty in forming emotional bonds and their tendency toward manipulation or deceit. However, maintaining relationships is possible with effort.

Recognizing Patterns – Be aware of tendencies like lying, manipulating, or pushing people away. Identifying these behaviors is the first step toward changing them.

Setting Boundaries – While people with ASPD may not feel emotional connections in the traditional sense, they can still respect boundaries and agreements in relationships.

Choosing Compatible Partners – Some individuals may tolerate or even appreciate certain ASPD traits, such as confidence and decisiveness. Seeking out partners who understand you can make relationships easier.

ii. Succeeding in the Workplace

Many people with ASPD thrive in high-pressure, competitive environments. However, impulsivity and rule-breaking can sometimes interfere with career success.

Finding the Right Job – Careers in law, business, sales, or military fields often reward traits associated with ASPD, such as assertiveness and risk-taking.

Managing Impulsivity – If reckless decision-making affects your work, developing self-discipline strategies (like setting personal rules or using logical checklists) can help.

Handling Authority Figures – Many with ASPD resist authority. Understanding when to push boundaries and when to comply can prevent unnecessary conflicts.

iii. Practical Tips for Daily Life

Develop Self-Discipline – Even if you don't feel guilt or remorse in the same way others do, following a set of personal rules can keep you out of trouble.

Use Logic to Navigate Social Situations – Instead of relying on emotional cues, analyzing situations rationally can help you determine how to act appropriately.

Keep a Low Profile When Necessary – If you struggle with impulsivity or aggression, learning when to walk away from conflicts can prevent unnecessary consequences.

Final Thoughts

If you suspect you have ASPD, your next steps depend on your goals. Some may seek professional diagnosis and treatment, while others may focus on self-awareness and personal management strategies. Regardless of which path you choose, understanding your tendencies and their effects on others can help you navigate life more effectively.

While ASPD comes with challenges, it is not a death sentence. Many people with ASPD lead successful, productive lives. The key is learning to manage your behaviors in a way that allows you to thrive while minimizing unnecessary conflict.

Would seeking a diagnosis benefit you, or would it create more problems? Can you improve your relationships and career prospects by making small behavioral adjustments? These are questions only you can answer. But by reading this book, you've already taken the first step toward understanding yourself better.

Chapter 15:

Support and Resources for Families & Loved Ones

Introduction

Living with someone who has Antisocial Personality Disorder (ASPD) can be an emotional and psychological roller coaster. It challenges family members, friends, and partners in ways that most people cannot fully understand unless they have experienced it firsthand. Navigating relationships with a person who has ASPD requires patience, resilience, and an understanding of the disorder's intricacies. Families, in particular, often find themselves at the crossroads of frustration, confusion, and helplessness. For those who love someone with ASPD, the need for support and resources cannot be overstated.

This chapter will explore essential strategies, coping mechanisms, and resources available for those affected by ASPD. It will cover how to communicate effectively with someone who has ASPD, how families can protect their mental and emotional health, and how to determine when to seek professional help. Ultimately, it will provide a roadmap to understanding how families and loved ones can work toward maintaining functional relationships, while still addressing the unique challenges that ASPD presents.

15.1 How to Communicate with Someone Who Has ASPD

Effective communication with someone who has ASPD can be one of the most daunting aspects of maintaining a relationship. Individuals with ASPD tend to lack the usual social cues that most people rely on, making it challenging for others to engage in meaningful dialogue. This is primarily due to the emotional and cognitive features of the disorder, which can make those with ASPD appear cold, manipulative, or indifferent to others' feelings. However, understanding these traits and developing communication strategies that work can improve interactions and help keep the relationship functional.

15.1.1 Be Direct and Clear

One of the most important aspects of communicating with someone who has ASPD is being straightforward. Avoid subtlety or implying things indirectly. People with ASPD tend to focus on the direct message and often lack patience for complex explanations or emotional nuance.

i. Use clear language: Rather than hinting at things or speaking in generalities, try to be as precise and concise as possible. Statements like "I need you to be on time for our meeting" are much more effective than saying "It would be nice if you could try to make it on time."

ii. Set boundaries clearly: Setting boundaries is critical in relationships with individuals who have ASPD. It's essential to clearly define your personal limits. For example, "It's not acceptable to speak to me like that" or "I will not tolerate being lied to."

iii. Avoid manipulation: Those with ASPD may engage in manipulative tactics. Stay firm and calm in your responses. If they try to shift the conversation or distract from the issue at hand, gently steer it back to the main point.

15.1.2 Stay Calm and Collected

People with ASPD often thrive in environments where they can provoke emotional reactions. Therefore, it's crucial for family members and loved ones to remain as calm and emotionally controlled as possible during conversations.

i. Don't engage in emotional manipulation: Avoid being pulled into emotional arguments or conflicts. People with ASPD may use emotional tactics to get what they want, so it's important to remain unaffected by these tactics.

ii. Keep your emotions in check: Displaying extreme emotions, whether frustration, anger, or sadness, may be interpreted as a sign of weakness or an opportunity for the person with ASPD to assert control. Instead, try to communicate logically, calmly, and with a controlled tone.

15.1.3 Understand Their Perspective, but Don't Excuse the Behavior

While understanding the nature of ASPD is essential, it's also important not to excuse problematic behavior. People with ASPD may have a different worldview, but that doesn't mean their actions should be tolerated or enabled.

i. Empathy vs. Enabling: Empathy involves understanding and acknowledging the feelings or circumstances of another person, while enabling means condoning harmful or destructive behavior. Try to understand the emotional experience behind their actions, but don't excuse behaviors that are hurtful or manipulative.

ii. Maintain healthy distance: While it's crucial to remain emotionally available, maintaining distance when needed can help keep the relationship balanced. Establishing personal space is essential for preserving your own well-being.

15.2 Coping Strategies for Families and Partners

Living with someone who has ASPD can be mentally and emotionally taxing. Families often find themselves caught between caring for the individual with the disorder while simultaneously protecting their own mental health. Without proper strategies in place, individuals can become worn out, stressed, and emotionally drained.

15.2.1 Self-Care and Mental Health

Family members of people with ASPD often neglect their own mental and emotional health in favor of trying to "fix" the individual with the disorder. However, self-care is crucial in maintaining any healthy relationship, especially in this context.

i. Recognize your own feelings: Family members need to acknowledge their own feelings and not suppress them. Feelings of anger, frustration, guilt, or sadness are valid, and it's important to process them in healthy ways.

ii. Seek personal therapy: Therapy or counseling for family members can be beneficial. Having a safe space to express feelings, develop coping skills, and receive guidance can make a significant difference in one's emotional well-being.

iii. Support groups: Connecting with others who have similar experiences can offer a sense of validation and reduce feelings of isolation. Support groups for families of individuals with ASPD or personality disorders can provide helpful insights, coping mechanisms, and emotional support.

15.2.2 Setting Realistic Expectations

One of the biggest challenges families face is the unrealistic expectation that their loved one with ASPD will change or conform to social norms. People with ASPD do not typically experience the same moral or ethical development as others, which means that change must come from their own desire or willingness.

i. Understand the limitations: Family members must recognize the limitations of treatment and behavior change. While therapy and support can help manage some symptoms, it is unlikely that someone with ASPD will undergo a complete transformation.

ii. Be realistic about boundaries: Set boundaries that are both firm and reasonable. It's essential to know what you can and cannot tolerate, and to communicate this clearly and consistently.

iii. Don't internalize their behavior: People with ASPD often do not understand the concept of empathy, and their actions are not a reflection of your worth or value. Don't internalize their behavior as a reflection of your relationship.

15.2.3 Building a Support Network

Creating a support network for both the individual with ASPD and their family is crucial for long-term success.

i. Involve extended family: Involving extended family members in discussions and decisions can help distribute the emotional burden and create a larger network of support.

ii. Educate others: Help others in your life understand ASPD so that they can offer support when needed. Educating friends, colleagues, and extended family members can provide a network that understands and doesn't judge.

iii. Prioritize your own well-being: Ultimately, you cannot support someone else effectively if you are not taking care of yourself. Prioritize your own mental and emotional health through therapy, hobbies, and social support.

15.3 When to Seek Help and How to Find It

Seeking professional help can be one of the most important steps for families and individuals navigating life with someone who has ASPD. Knowing when and how to seek help is vital for everyone's well-being.

15.3.1 Seeking Professional Therapy or Counseling

i. Individual therapy: Therapy for family members can help manage stress, guilt, and emotional exhaustion. Speaking with a therapist about personal experiences can provide coping strategies and prevent burnout.

ii. Couples therapy: In some cases, couples therapy might be beneficial if the person with ASPD is willing to engage. However, this should be approached cautiously and with the understanding that ASPD behaviors may not be easily altered.

iii. Family therapy: Family therapy can also be an option for addressing relationship dynamics and helping family members understand how to communicate effectively with the person with ASPD.

15.3.2 When the Situation Becomes Dangerous

i. Recognize the signs of escalating behavior: If the person with ASPD begins to display violent, abusive, or dangerous behavior, seeking professional help or involving law enforcement may be necessary for everyone's safety.

ii. Crisis intervention services: If the situation escalates, seeking crisis intervention services may help provide immediate support. This can prevent harm and guide the family in developing a long-term plan for dealing with the behavior.

iii. Protecting children and vulnerable individuals: Families with children or vulnerable members may need to take extra precautions to ensure their safety. In these cases, involving professionals or even considering a temporary separation might be necessary.

Conclusion

Supporting a loved one with ASPD is undoubtedly challenging, but it is not impossible. By understanding the disorder, setting clear boundaries, practicing self-care, and seeking professional help when needed, families can navigate the complexities of living with someone who has ASPD. It requires patience, perseverance, and a deep commitment to self-preservation while still offering the support that the individual with ASPD may need.

Building a functional life with ASPD is not about changing the person, but about managing the disorder's impact on the relationships and maintaining one's own emotional health. Resources, therapy, and a strong support network are crucial to making this journey less isolating and more manageable for everyone involved.

Bonus Section:

Further Exploration (Appendix or Extra Content)

The Evolution of ASPD in Psychiatry – How ASPD Has Been Defined Over Time

Antisocial Personality Disorder (ASPD) has evolved significantly in its conceptualization and classification within psychiatric literature. Over time, shifts in our understanding of human behavior, the refinement of diagnostic criteria, and the advent of new research methodologies have all contributed to how we define and diagnose ASPD today. This section traces the major milestones in the development of ASPD as a disorder.

i.1 From Moral Insanity to Psychopathy

The earliest conceptions of what would later become ASPD emerged in the 19th century. The term moral insanity was coined by British psychiatrist Henry Maudsley in the mid-1800s. He used the term to describe individuals who exhibited behaviors such as criminality, irresponsibility, and lack of empathy, but without showing the typical signs of mental illness such as delusions or hallucinations. These individuals were thought to be morally defective, but not mentally ill in the conventional sense.

As psychiatry progressed, this concept evolved into what was referred to as psychopathy. Psychopathy became associated with a more specific set of traits, including a lack of empathy, disregard for social norms, manipulativeness, and impulsivity. Psychopathy was thought to be a personality disorder that involved inherent character flaws, making individuals more likely to engage in criminal or antisocial behaviors. However, psychopathy was not yet formally recognized in diagnostic manuals, and the concept remained largely theoretical.

i.2 The Birth of ASPD

The formalization of ASPD as a diagnostic category began with the publication of the Diagnostic and Statistical Manual of Mental Disorders (DSM) by the American Psychiatric Association. In the 1980s, the DSM-III included ASPD as an official diagnosis, marking a shift away from the vague and outdated concept of moral insanity or psychopathy. The diagnostic criteria for ASPD were based on behavioral patterns that indicated chronic disregard for the rights of others, as well as a consistent pattern of deceit, manipulation, and impulsivity.

ASPD's introduction in the DSM-III represented a move towards a more structured and clinical approach to understanding antisocial behavior. The diagnosis was not based on an individual's level of empathy or morality, but rather their consistent pattern of criminality and manipulation.

i.3 The DSM-IV and DSM-5: Refining the Diagnosis

The DSM-IV (published in 1994) and the DSM-5 (published in 2013) made refinements to the definition and diagnostic criteria of ASPD. The most significant change was the clearer distinction between psychopathy and ASPD. While ASPD remained the diagnostic category, psychopathy was increasingly understood as a more specific and severe personality disorder often used in forensic contexts.

The DSM-5 emphasizes behaviors such as repeated violation of societal norms, impulsivity, irritability, and lack of remorse. It includes a diagnostic criterion that states the individual must have a history of conduct disorder symptoms before the age of 15, which helps to distinguish ASPD from other personality disorders and developmental disorders.

i.4 ASPD in Modern Psychiatry

Today, ASPD is recognized as one of the most challenging personality disorders to treat. It is closely linked with other mental health issues such as substance abuse, anxiety disorders, and depression. Treatment options are often limited, and successful outcomes are rare, although research into effective therapies, including cognitive behavioral therapy (CBT) and dialectical behavior therapy (DBT), is ongoing. ASPD remains a highly stigmatized disorder, often associated with criminal behavior and manipulation, although not all individuals diagnosed with ASPD engage in illegal activities or have violent tendencies.

ASPD vs. Other Personality Disorders – Comparing Borderline, Narcissistic, and Antisocial Traits

ASPD shares some similarities with other personality disorders, particularly Borderline Personality Disorder (BPD) and Narcissistic Personality Disorder (NPD). However, there are key differences that help distinguish ASPD from these other disorders. Understanding these distinctions is crucial for clinicians and those affected by these disorders, as it aids in appropriate diagnosis and treatment.

ii.1 Borderline Personality Disorder (BPD)

BPD is often confused with ASPD because both disorders involve impulsive behaviors and difficulty with interpersonal relationships. However, the core features of BPD and ASPD differ significantly:

Emotional Instability: BPD is primarily characterized by emotional instability and intense fear of abandonment, while ASPD is characterized by disregard for others' rights and a pattern of deceitful and manipulative behaviors.

Self-Image: Individuals with BPD often struggle with identity disturbance and have an unstable sense of self, whereas those with ASPD are more likely to exhibit egocentric behavior and lack empathy.

Relationship Patterns: People with BPD may have intense, volatile relationships and a history of self-harm, while individuals with ASPD may engage in manipulative, exploitative relationships with little regard for the feelings or well-being of others.

Despite these differences, both disorders can be disruptive to individuals' lives and relationships. However, the root causes and the way in which symptoms manifest are significantly different.

ii.2 Narcissistic Personality Disorder (NPD)

NPD and ASPD share a lack of empathy and disregard for the feelings of others, but they differ in their core motivations and behaviors:

Need for Admiration: Individuals with NPD typically crave admiration and validation, often displaying grandiosity and a sense of entitlement. In contrast, those with ASPD seek to exploit and manipulate others for personal gain, with little to no concern for how their actions affect others.

Sense of Superiority: People with NPD may have an inflated sense of self-importance but are often vulnerable to criticism or rejection. In contrast, individuals with ASPD often lack remorse and view their behavior as justified, showing little to no vulnerability to external judgment.

Emotional Regulation: People with ASPD tend to be more impulsive, aggressive, and reactive, while those with NPD may have more controlled behaviors, masking their insecurities behind a facade of confidence.

Understanding these distinctions is crucial when diagnosing and treating individuals with personality disorders, as it helps to tailor therapeutic interventions more effectively.

ii.3 Similarities Between ASPD, BPD, and NPD

While each of these disorders has its distinct features, they do share some overlapping traits, such as:

Difficulty in Relationships: All three disorders can result in dysfunctional interpersonal relationships, though the underlying reasons vary (e.g., fear of abandonment in BPD, manipulation in ASPD, and admiration-seeking in NPD).

Impaired Empathy: A lack of empathy is a hallmark of both ASPD and NPD, though those with BPD may struggle with emotional regulation and react impulsively in relationships rather than displaying consistent disregard for others.

Recommended Books, Studies, and Documentaries – Further Reading for Curious Minds

For those interested in diving deeper into the topic of ASPD, here are some recommended resources—books, studies, and documentaries—that provide further insight into the complexities of the disorder.

iii.1 Recommended Books

1. "The Sociopath Next Door" by Martha Stout This book offers a look into the lives of people who may not fit the clinical definition of ASPD but exhibit sociopathic traits. Stout explores how sociopaths blend into society and the impact of their behavior on others.
2. "Without Conscience: The Disturbing World of the Psychopaths Among Us" by Robert Hare Written by a leading expert in psychopathy, this book provides a detailed examination of psychopathy and its distinction from ASPD. It also offers insights into how individuals with psychopathy interact with the world and the challenges they present to society.
3. "The Psychopath Test" by Jon Ronson This book is a compelling journey through the world of psychopathy and ASPD. Ronson explores the concept of psychopathy, how it's diagnosed, and the ethical implications of labeling someone as a psychopath.

iii.2 Recommended Studies

1. "A Comprehensive Review of Antisocial Personality Disorder" by Scott O. Lilienfeld This study provides an in-depth review of ASPD, including its diagnostic criteria, treatment options, and the ongoing challenges in understanding the disorder from a scientific perspective.
2. "Neurobiological Bases of Antisocial Behavior" by Adrian Raine Raine's research focuses on the neurological factors that contribute to ASPD, offering insights into how brain abnormalities may underlie behaviors such as aggression, impulsivity, and lack of empathy.

iii.3 Recommended Documentaries

1. "The Psychopath Test" (2011) This documentary, based on Jon Ronson's book, takes viewers on a journey into the world of psychopathy, offering a closer look at how individuals with ASPD and psychopathy are diagnosed and treated.
2. "The Mind of a Monster" (2014) A documentary exploring the psychology of serial killers and criminals with ASPD traits. It provides a chilling look at how individuals with ASPD can manipulate and deceive others, often blending into society unnoticed.
3. "The Narcissist Next Door" (2015) This documentary delves into the traits of narcissism and explores the overlap between narcissistic personality disorder and ASPD, focusing on how individuals with these disorders navigate personal relationships and social structures.

Conclusion:

A New Perspective on ASPD

Moving Beyond the Stereotypes

Throughout this book, we've examined the complexities of Antisocial Personality Disorder (ASPD), diving deep into its clinical foundations, its psychological and societal implications, and its representation in the media. One of the key takeaways from our exploration is the urgent need to move beyond the stereotypes that often cloud our understanding of this disorder.

The term "antisocial" conjures up images of violent criminals, manipulators, and cold-hearted individuals who derive pleasure from causing harm to others. While these behaviors can indeed be present in some individuals with ASPD, they represent only one aspect of a much broader, more nuanced reality. The disorder manifests differently across individuals, and many with ASPD are not violent nor criminal in their actions. Understanding this complexity is essential in fostering a more accurate and empathetic view of those with ASPD.

i.1 The Media's Role in Shaping Our Perceptions

The media plays a significant role in perpetuating negative stereotypes about ASPD. Movies, television shows, and news outlets frequently depict individuals with ASPD as dangerous, manipulative, and devoid of any moral compass. This portrayal has contributed to widespread fear and misunderstanding.

For instance, films featuring psychopathic characters—such as those based on real-life criminals—often portray these individuals as highly intelligent, charming, and, ultimately, dangerous. While some with ASPD may display these traits, it is important to remember that not everyone with ASPD engages in harmful or criminal behavior. The overwhelming majority of individuals with ASPD live outside the criminal justice system, and many simply struggle with interpersonal relationships and emotional regulation.

i.2 Moving Toward Compassionate Understanding

It is crucial to approach ASPD not with fear, but with an understanding rooted in both clinical insight and human empathy. People with ASPD are often the product of complex interactions between genetics, early trauma, environmental factors, and their own personal struggles. They are individuals with histories, experiences, and challenges, not just labels.

This shift in perspective can help dismantle the stigma surrounding ASPD and promote more compassionate and effective interventions. By recognizing that ASPD, like other mental health disorders, exists on a spectrum, and that its manifestations can vary widely, we can create a more inclusive, supportive society for those affected by it.

Understanding, Not Fear

The journey through understanding ASPD is one of nuance, complexity, and emotional intelligence. To truly engage with the issue, we must move past fear-based reactions to a stance of understanding and empathy.

ii.1 The Need for Education and Awareness

One of the most important steps in creating a more empathetic and informed society is education. The more we learn about ASPD—its origins, symptoms, treatment options, and its many manifestations—the less we will rely on harmful stereotypes. Knowledge is the antidote to fear, and the more people are informed about ASPD, the better equipped they will be to interact with, support, and help those who live with the disorder.

Educational initiatives can also help in reducing the stigma faced by individuals with ASPD. Currently, many people with ASPD avoid seeking help due to the fear of being labeled or misunderstood. These individuals may silently suffer, unable to access the resources they need because of societal prejudice. A more open-minded, well-informed public will create an environment where people can seek the help they need without fear of judgment.

ii.2 Therapy and Treatment: A Path to Change

As discussed throughout this book, ASPD is not a condition that is easily "cured," but with proper treatment and support, it is possible for individuals to manage their symptoms and lead functional, fulfilling lives. Therapy—particularly Cognitive Behavioral Therapy (CBT) and Dialectical Behavior Therapy (DBT)—has shown promise in helping individuals with ASPD develop better coping strategies, emotional regulation, and interpersonal skills.

For those affected by ASPD, understanding the disorder is the first step in self-improvement. With the right therapeutic support, individuals with ASPD can work toward changing maladaptive patterns of behavior and building healthier relationships.

Final Thoughts on the Label "Antisocial"

The label "antisocial" itself is a double-edged sword. On one hand, it serves as a clinical descriptor, helping professionals to identify a specific set of traits and behaviors that indicate the presence of ASPD. On the other hand, this label carries a heavy stigma, often used as a shorthand for "dangerous" or "evil," regardless of the individual's actual behavior or capacity for change.

iii.1 The Problem with Labels

While labels can be useful in diagnosing and treating disorders, they also carry significant weight in how we perceive and interact with people. Labels can be limiting, defining individuals solely by their disorder and reducing their identity to a single diagnostic category. This is particularly problematic with ASPD, where the label may overshadow the person's humanity and complexities. People with ASPD are often reduced to nothing more than their most negative traits, and this can exacerbate feelings of alienation and hopelessness.

iii.2 The Power of Understanding the Whole Person

Instead of focusing solely on the label of "antisocial," we should strive to see the whole person—their background, struggles, and potential for growth. Many individuals with ASPD have experienced trauma, neglect, and adverse circumstances that shaped their development. They are not inherently "bad" or "evil"; they are human beings with the capacity for change, given the right support and treatment.

Ultimately, the goal should not be to simply remove the label of ASPD but to approach individuals with compassion and understanding. We must also recognize that the label is not a permanent verdict on their identity. Like anyone else, those with ASPD can grow, change, and improve their lives.

Moving Toward a Better Future

The future of ASPD diagnosis, treatment, and societal acceptance hinges on several factors:

1. Increased Research: Continued research into the neurological and environmental causes of ASPD will help improve our understanding of the disorder and lead to better treatments.
2. More Effective Interventions: As we gain more insight into ASPD, treatment modalities will continue to evolve, becoming more effective at helping individuals manage their symptoms and live fulfilling lives.
3. Public Education and Awareness: Education campaigns aimed at reducing stigma and increasing understanding of ASPD can foster greater empathy and support for individuals living with the disorder.
4. Compassionate Care: Mental health professionals, caregivers, and family members must provide compassionate care to individuals with

ASPD, seeing them not as "lost causes" but as people who deserve understanding and support.

By embracing a more compassionate, informed approach to ASPD, we can help individuals with this disorder achieve better outcomes, while also enriching our society as a whole. The goal should always be to understand, not fear, and to recognize the full humanity of those affected by ASPD.

As we conclude this exploration of Antisocial Personality Disorder, we are reminded that the label "antisocial" does not define a person's entire being. Understanding ASPD as a complex, multifaceted disorder opens the door to greater empathy, better treatment options, and ultimately, a world in which individuals with ASPD can lead meaningful, productive lives. The final thought is simple: people with ASPD, like anyone else, are more than their disorder. They are capable of growth, change, and connection—if only we give them the chance.

www.ingramcontent.com/pod-product-compliance
Lightning Source LLC
LaVergne TN
LVHW020442070526
838199LV00063B/4814